One Win A Day

Charlotte Greedy is a mum of two who is best known as @missgreedyshome. She creates relatable and funny content around her home and family life, as well as sharing what she's loving in the beauty, fashion, and lifestyle sector. She has also used her platform to raise money for mental health charities. She lives in Wales with her fiancée Harriet, her two children Enzo and Brody, and her fur babies Beau, Kobe and Minnie. Her first book, *You Do You*, was a *Sunday Times* bestseller.

This is for all you beautiful humans out there who need a little help with self-love or self-care. Let's do one win a day together, celebrating every win, no matter how small.

TRANSWORLD PUBLISHERS
Penguin Random House, One Embassy Gardens, 8 Viaduct Gardens,
London SW11 7BW
www.penguin.co.uk

Transworld is part of the Penguin Random House group of companies
whose addresses can be found at global.penguinrandomhouse.com

Penguin
Random House
UK

First published in Great Britain in 2023 by Bantam
an imprint of Transworld Publishers

A CIP catalogue record for this book
is available from the British Library.

ISBN 9780857505736

Design by Louise Evans louiseevans.design
Printed and bound in Great Britain by Clays Ltd, Elcograf S.p.A.

The authorized representative in the EEA is Penguin Random House Ireland,
Morrison Chambers, 32 Nassau Street, Dublin D02 YH68.

Penguin Random House is committed to a sustainable future for our
business, our readers and our planet. This book is made from Forest
Stewardship Council® certified paper.

MIX
Paper | Supporting
responsible forestry
FSC
www.fsc.org   FSC® C018179

Charlotte Greedy

One Win A Day

365 little steps to make a big difference

bantam

Hi guys!

Can I just start us off by saying one thing?

You are AMAZING.

You might not feel it every day – who does? You probably have days where you feel down or frazzled, or you're struggling with your mental health. You might feel disorganized or be in a bad mood because you forgot your umbrella and it rained, or you got a parking ticket. That's OK.

But you are still amazing!

There is so much pressure on us – to have the perfect partner, kids, home or job. All while looking perfect too, obviously. But that's not how life works. All that pressure to be constantly achieving is not realistic and it's not healthy. It's actually the simple, everyday wins that add up to something real – you feeling happy and confident in your own brain.

A win isn't some big award or promotion. It's anything that makes you feel good. It's reminding yourself to take the time to rest, to re-energize and be in the moment. It's spending time with your friends, your family, your fur babies. It's getting those annoying chores ticked off the list and rewarding yourself with crisps and some episodes of your favourite TV programme. It's being kind to yourself.

Not every single thing on every single page is going to change your life – it's actually sort of the opposite. They are things that help me and I hope they help you too. They are practical ways to help you take time out, to remember to focus on yourself, and to remind you to appreciate yourself and how amazing you are. And obviously I'm really hoping you'll have fun doing them!

My dream is that by challenging you to do one small thing FOR YOU every day, the little things in these pages will mean something much bigger. When we know ourselves really well and we allow ourselves to dream, to plan, to be who we want to be, THAT'S when we get the life we love and we value everything we have. It's not about what anyone else thinks or about things you 'should' be doing to tick boxes. There is no pressure here. I want you to be blown away by how capable and confident you can be. And you can do that one win at a time.

How to use this book

There are 365 entries in this book (yep – the same number as days in a year – in a leap year you can give yourself one day off. Just one!), but you don't have to start it on any particular day. If you're a 1st January person, fired up with shiny resolutions, then that's great – you do you! But for many of us, January comes with too much pressure to start a load of new habits (and too much crap, depressing weather, in the UK at least!). So if you're ready to start something new on 25th April or 12th November that's totally fine. I'll be here when you're ready.

Ideally, I'd like you to start at the beginning of the book and work through, day by day. On some days you'll find a challenge – to push yourself a little bit, to get on with something you've been meaning to do, to try something new. On others I'll be encouraging you to take a moment for yourself, to step away from your phone, to think about all the great things you already have in your life. And sometimes it's just about giving yourself a treat or a reward – because you absolutely bloody deserve it! I know that some of these will appeal more to you than others. But I'd love it if you would at least give each one a go.

Along the way, we have some challenges that come up regularly:

PICK A THEME

Every four weeks or so, I'm going to ask you to pick something to focus on for the upcoming month. It might be practical, like researching new jobs or getting a DIY project finished, or something more emotional, such as friendship or trying new things. Maybe there's an area of your life you feel you're neglecting and you want to change that. Some themes you choose will be specific and others might not.

Basically, it's a chance for you to decide what's important to you right now and to prioritize it. The thing to remember is that you should choose each theme because it's something you care about, rather than because of what anyone else thinks.

Maybe focusing on the theme will mean you end up doing lots of work in that area. Or it might just be something you think about more. Either way, two weeks in, I'll check in to give you a chance to think about how it's going.

You can choose anything you want. Here are some examples:

- ★ Work
- ★ Eating better
- ★ Good mental health habits
- ★ Seeing friends more

- ★ Making travel plans
- ★ Self-confidence
- ★ Family time
- ★ Body confidence
- ★ Making time to be creative
- ★ New experiences

Make it as specific as you like. This is an opportunity to consider what really matters to you and write it in capital letters on a Post-it note in your brain.

CELEBRATE!

Every four weeks, there's also a chance for you to focus on all the things that have gone well and give yourself a big round of applause. Sometimes when we feel down or a bit stuck we brush over all the good things and let our brains get stuck on what we haven't managed to do. But no matter how big or small, it's important to remember that A WIN IS A WIN!

FOCUS WEEKS

There are some areas of life that I have struggled with in the past (and still struggle with) and I know from talking to hundreds of other people on social media that I am not the only one. These areas deserve a bit of extra attention. So you'll find that there are whole weeks when we'll focus specifically on self-confidence, body confidence, mental health, kindness and heroes – because you can be the hero you need in your life!

VISION BOARDS

Imagination is a very powerful thing. You can't do anything unless you can imagine it first. Our dreams can also teach us what our heart most wants. And not only is daydreaming fun, but sometimes dreams lead to inspiration, inspiration leads to ideas, and ideas may lead to ACTION! (Or sometimes dreams are just dreams, and that's cool too.) Vision boards are a way of capturing this – and a chance to get a bit creative, too.

TODAY, I AM GRATEFUL FOR . . .

And finally, as well as remembering to celebrate the good things we've done and enjoyed, it's so great to stop and think about what we already have. I believe that you CAN go out and get the life you want – but it's not just about the future, it's about appreciating the lovely things in the here and now.

 What are the stars for?

You'll notice that there are little stars in the corners of the pages. This is a way to mark any of the days that particularly worked for you or you want to come back to try. That's great! Just colour them in, any colour you like, and you'll be able to flick back to them whenever you want.

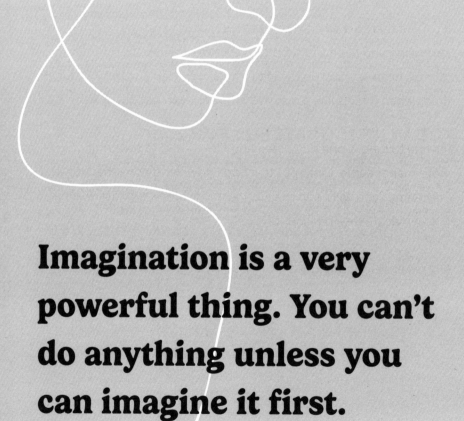

Imagination is a very powerful thing. You can't do anything unless you can imagine it first.

Are you ready to start?

Before you turn the page and make a start, I just want to say one last, really important, thing.

It's OK if there's a day, a week, even a month when you are struggling and even the simplest task feels too much. This happens to me. I have so much in my life that I am grateful for, but I still have times when it feels like a massive effort to even get out of bed.

It's fine to ignore one day's idea and flick ahead to something more manageable. Or to put this book down and come back to it. Sometimes you will need to give yourself a break and just do what you can do. Please be kind to you.

OK. Shall we get going?!

All about you

Ready to start? OK, first things first. Your challenge today is simply to think about all the things that are important to you. What is it that makes you you? The questions below might help you, but the main thing is just to write what you feel.

Who in your life are you closest to? What do you particularly value about them?

_____

_____

What causes do you care most about?

_____

_____

What are you happiest doing?

_____

_____

Are you an indoors or an outdoors person?

_____

_____

Do you like to travel or is home where your heart is?

_____

_____

What really makes you laugh?

_____

_____

What qualities do you most value in other people?

_____

_____

And in yourself?

_____

_____

Getting to know yourself better is always a win – and it's a great starting point for the journey we're about to go on together!

2

Choose your theme #1

Today you're going to pick your first theme. We'll be picking something different every four weeks to focus on. You might like to look back to your 'All about you' list from yesterday for inspiration. What needs some thought or more space in your life? Find a piece of paper, write it down and stick it somewhere you'll see it – like over the kettle or on the bathroom mirror. Try to spend at least a few minutes each day thinking about why whatever you've chosen is important to you right now (like while the kettle is boiling or you are brushing your teeth!) and what actions you might like to take.

MY THEME IS

3   A gift for Future You

Find an envelope and some cash. It doesn't have to be much – two quid, a fiver, a tenner if you want. Put the money in the envelope and write your own name on the front. Now tuck it away somewhere it won't get lost but where you won't see it all the time – like a bedside drawer.

If you've had a really bad day, or you're feeling low or hormonal, you can go find this money and buy yourself a little present. Bubble bath, face cream, a family-sized bar of chocolate. Whatever it is your bruised heart or tired brain needs that day. You could also include a little note to Future You in the envelope with some words you might want to hear when things haven't gone so well.

4   Play a board game

I bet you have one in the cupboard somewhere! Put your phone in a drawer and challenge someone to the Ludo/Cluedo/Monopoly match of their lives. This is weirdly great for mindfulness – it's literally impossible not to be 'present in the moment' when trying to remove a block from a wobbly Jenga tower!

5 Send a message to someone you haven't spoken to for a while

Life gets so busy and all of a sudden you realize it's been ages since you've been in touch with a friend. Go through your contacts today – who would you love a good chat with? Send them a message, even if it's just saying hi and asking how they are. You might make their day!

6 Sort out a drawer

When you don't feel like you can declutter your brain, sorting out something in the physical world can be highly satisfying. Whether it's that random bits-and-bobs drawer in the kitchen (every kitchen has one!) or a tangle of jewellery and make-up in a bedside table, go grab it now. Throw away what needs to go, rehome anything that doesn't live there and clean out the dust from the corners. It will take you less than ten minutes today and restore a bit of calming order in a small corner of your world.

7 Feel a bit uncomfortable and do it anyway

There's a famous saying: 'Do one thing that scares you every day.' That's great if you can do it, but even if you can't you can still challenge yourself to do something that feels on the edge of your comfort zone. So today I would love you to think of three things that make you uncomfortable or a bit nervous that you can try to do this week. Write them down below and have a think about when you might do them. Maybe it's asking for some help or careers advice at college, speaking up at a meeting, asking someone out for a drink . . . Anything you like!

1 _____

_____

2 _____

_____

3 _____

_____

8 Help a stranger

You're going to have to keep your eyes peeled for this one. Sometimes I like to pay for the coffee order of the car behind me at the drive-thru. But helping doesn't have to involve money. Help someone carry something heavy, let them go in front of you in a queue if you can tell they are in a rush, entertain a crying child on the train to help out a tired parent. The good thing about this challenge is that it makes you really pay attention to the people around you so you notice when they might need a hand. Kindness costs nothing, guys!

9 Do a knicker cull

If you have a beautiful collection of pretty matching underwear, then I am very jealous – I'm a Bridget Jones girl through and through. For everyone who's like me, now is the time to get rid of our old, saggy, holey knickers. And *particularly* the uncomfy ones. You can keep a few of the massive granny pairs you wear when you're on your period, but anything that slides down or rides up(!) should go. You are a busy and brilliant woman who does not need to be troubled by uncomfortable underwear.

10 Plan something fun

Today, I challenge you to get something in the diary to look forward to. It could be anything from a girls' dinner out to meeting a friend for a walk or a coffee. It's so easy to get caught up with all the things on the to-do list and not make the time for the people we love and like a lot. Don't rely on other people to make a date or think, *Well, they would have contacted me if they wanted to do something*. I'm guilty of sometimes thinking like that, but the fact is that someone has to be the first to reach out – so why not you?

11 Stretch

This is such a good thing to do if you are sat at a desk all day for work, or for anyone really. A full body stretch is a great way to release tension and say thank you to your muscles and joints for all the hard work they do. As a starting point, stand on your tiptoes and reach for the sky. Take a deep breath in and exhale as you slowly lower your arms and bend forward so your arms hang loosely in front of you. There are lots of videos online – have a look for one that feels right for you.

12 Get dressed up for no reason, part one . . .

Before you go to bed tonight, I want you to do two things:

1 Get one of your favourite outfits out of the wardrobe and lay it or hang it where you'll see it when you wake up. Your best underwear too, and any accessories you want to wear with it. The whole deal, top to toe.

2 Set the alarm fifteen minutes earlier than usual.

13 Get dressed up for no reason, part two

When you wake up today, use that extra fifteen minutes to focus on your skincare, your make-up (if you wear it) and/or your hair. Put on that great outfit and before you walk out the door, remember to tell yourself you look bloody beautiful today. Usually, we put the extra effort in because we're going somewhere special. Today, it's all for you and only for you. When you get into bed tonight, think about how your day was and how setting aside that fifteen minutes to focus on yourself made you feel.

It's so easy to get caught up with all the things on the to-do list and not make the time for the people we love.

14 TWO-WEEK CHECK-IN!

You are halfway through your theme of the month.
How do you think it's going? Have you found time to
reflect on it? Today, think about if there is any practical
action you'd like to take, if you haven't already. Is there
anything you'd like to try out or change?

15 Today, I am grateful for . . .

Every so often we are going to pause so you can take
a moment to think about all the things you are grateful
for right now. This is something I do frequently as I
think it's easy to be focused on where we want to
get to next and forget about all the wonderful things
around us right now. So in the space below, make a list
of all the little (and big!) things that bring you joy and
make your world go round.

_____

_____

_____

_____

16 Give yourself a pedicure

Rummage in the cupboard for anything you can find to use – foot cream, nail files, cuticle sticks, etc. – and give those poor tired feet some love today.

17 Cook something different

We all get a bit stuck in a rut in the kitchen, particularly when we're busy, but it's good to change things up. It doesn't have to be anything complicated or time consuming, and it doesn't even have to be cooked from scratch. Just something that's not your default-mode jacket potato or pasta bake.

18 Break the routine

Think about the small things you do every day. How can you switch something up today? Can you take a different route to work? Eat lunch in the park? Have a spontaneous dinner out? Watch the sunset rather than sit in front of the TV? A break in your routine can help you get out of a rut.

19   Do the thing

What boring thing have you been putting off for weeks? I am such a pro at this kind of procrastination! There's bound to be something! Well, today is the day. Maybe it's replacing a lightbulb that's been out for ages, booking the dentist or cleaning the oven. Take a moment to imagine how good it will feel when it's out of the way and – before you have the chance to talk yourself out of it – go get it done! Honestly, you'll get a buzz from ticking it off the list (and rewarding yourself afterwards with a treat of your choice!).

HERO WEEK

Go get your cape, because for the next few days we're going to be thinking about our heroes – the people we admire – but also how we can be our own hero . . .

(20) Let me be your hero

Who are your heroes? Which well-known people – fictional or real – do you look up to or admire for what they have achieved? Make a list and also write down what you find most inspiring about them.

_____

_____

_____

_____

_____

_____

_____

_____

_____

21 The real heroes

Now think about the people you know who you think are heroic or have superpowers. Which of your friends and family are inspiring and why? It doesn't have to be people you still know; you can include people from your past, too. Like an amazing teacher you once had or someone who was really brave in the face of illness or pain. Again, write a list and include what you find inspiring about them. Maybe even tell the person if you want to – it might make their day.

_____

_____

_____

_____

_____

_____

_____

(22) What are your superpowers?

Right, time to ditch the modesty! What are you really bloody good at? What do your friends and family admire and value you for? What can you do that other people seem to struggle with? There are eight lines below but write as many as you like, and they can be ANYTHING – big or small! Maybe you're a great cook, or a supportive friend, or you're really good at finding lost things or bargains on Amazon. Anything! We spend too much time thinking about what other people are good at and we totally take our own talents for granted.

1 _____

2 _____

3 _____

4 _____

5 _____

6 _____

7 _____

8 _____

23 What superpowers would you like to have?

Don't think about whether you believe this is something you could be good at – just write down what you would *like* to be good at. Keep it fairly realistic, though – actual superpowers like flying or X-ray vision might be a bit ambitious.

1 _____

2 _____

3 _____

24 Feel the power

Yesterday, you thought about some superpowers you would love to have. Well, today let's think about how you are going to get them! Just pick one or two and think about small things you can do to get better at them. Do you need more practice? Is there someone in your life who is great at this thing who could help you? Do you need to learn a new skill?

(25) Hi there, Wonder Woman!

I bet there have been times in your life when you have flown in to the rescue or faced something difficult and surprised yourself with your amazing strength. Write down two or three examples below and think about: What skills or strengths helped you? How did it feel? What do you think this shows you about your superpowers, about what you are capable of?

_____

_____

_____

_____

_____

_____

_____

_____

26 Your secret alter-ego

So, over the past week, you have thought about who
your heroes are and why, what your superpowers are
(and what you would like them to be), and reflected
on times you were a hero. Now I want you to draw
yourself as a superhero! Design an awesome outfit
and around your drawing add words or phrases
representing your special powers. Come up with
a bad-ass name for your alter-ego. When you find
yourself struggling in the future you can ask yourself,
'What would _____ do in this situation?' Take a picture
on your phone so they are always with you!

27 Celebrate!

We've now been doing one win a day for almost four weeks! How has it been for you? Today, I want you to think about all the things that have felt good this month. I don't care if they are big or small. I mean, obviously yay for you if you got a new job, but you are also bloody brilliant if you remembered to put the bins out. And not just things you achieved: what was just *good*? Getting a compliment on your work? Or on your outfit? Getting together with the girls? Really think about your favourite things you've done since you started the book and write them below.

_____

_____

_____

_____

_____

_____

_____

_____

Choose your theme #2

Ready for another theme? How did the spot you picked to display your theme work out for you last time? Did you see if often enough? If not, think about sticking up the piece of paper with your theme written on it somewhere different this time.

MY THEME IS

_____

29 Go for a walk

Yes, even if it's raining! You've got a brolly, haven't you? Ideally, it won't be to the shop or to run an errand – just a walk for the sake of a walk. Try to notice as much as you can. Which house has the best garden? Can you hear birds, music? What does the sky look like today? Leave your headphones (even your phone!) at home. This walk is for you, your brain and your five senses only.

30 Reboot the snacks

Women are constantly being told what they should and shouldn't be eating, based on how our bodies are 'supposed' to look, and I am definitely not here to add to that pile of crap. However, looking after our bodies so they can look after us *is* important. Particularly as good gut health is increasingly being linked by some scientists to good mental health. You don't have to ditch the biscuits altogether; instead, make a list on your phone of all the things you like to snack on that are more nutritious and less sugary as a reminder next time you are in the supermarket. If you have these to hand, you might find you naturally reach for the crisps and chocolate less often.

31 Make time for your almost-friends

Who are your almost-friends? Is there anyone in your life you really like but don't yet know that well? Maybe a neighbour you always stop to chat to, a colleague who seems really nice, a friend of a friend who you often run into . . . Could you invite your neighbour in for a coffee? Suggest to your colleague that you eat lunch together? Invite the friend of a friend to a gathering or to the pub for a drink? If we don't make the effort to reach out, we'll never get to know anyone new. And who knows, it could mean a lot to that person that someone bothered to make the effort. You don't have to become BFFs – the point is just to try and put yourself out there. Two of my best friends I didn't even know a couple of years ago.

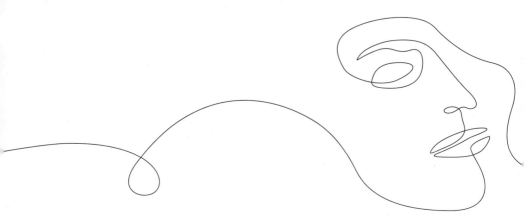

32 Breathe

Yes, I know you are doing it already or you'd be dead! Hear me out. If you suffer from anxiety or have ever had panic attacks you might know this one, but it's a handy technique for anyone to be aware of. It's called box breathing.

★ Gently breathe in for the count of four.

★ Hold your breath for four.

★ Breathe out for a count of four.

★ Hold it there for the count of four before breathing in again.

★ Do this four times, or more if you need.

It's a really good way of calming yourself down after something really stressful happens and for stopping your heart from racing.

VISION BOARD!
Holidays . . .

Today, I want you to dream about your perfect holiday. Who's there? Where are you? What are you doing? Think about the details too – like the weather and what you are eating. Dream away and then describe the scene below:

34 The happiness bank

Today, I want you to think of as many things as you can that make you feel calm or cheer you up. Is there a friend who always makes you laugh? A dog you can *cwtch*? Do you find a walk, a run or doing something creative resets you? When we are feeling a bit crap, then we don't always remember what makes us feel good, but if you write it here you'll always have a reminder. Take a picture on your phone or colour this page's star with a highlighter so you can find it easily.

_____

_____

_____

_____

35 Three five-minute jobs

Ticking something off the to-do list is so, so satisfying. For a little hit of motivation, think of three five-minute jobs that have been outstanding for a while and bump them up the list. Book a haircut, buy a new mop, hang that picture . . . Just get them done today and give yourself a big fat tick for each.

36 Write a letter

I mean, no, I don't know how people coped when the only way to communicate was to write to someone and wait two days for an answer either. But there's something really lovely about taking the time to write down a message on paper rather than tapping out a few emojis. It doesn't have to be long or serious. It could be a funny note to your partner, a card to a friend who has been through a tough time, or even a letter to your son or daughter to tell them you love them and are proud of them. The point is to sit down with a pen and paper and think about what you want to say.

37 Have a phone-free evening

Before you sit down for dinner, turn your phone to silent and put it in a drawer. So no scrolling, no messaging for a whole evening. Just focus on what you are doing and the people you are with. Yes, we love our phones, but they take us out of the moment and are not always good for our brains.

(NB: Most smartphones have a feature where you can allow certain numbers to ring even if your phone is on silent or do not disturb mode. Handy if you want some phone downtime but you are a carer for someone or need to know if the kids' school gets in touch.)

38 Make a fakeaway

Anyone who knows me will know I'm an absolute sucker for a takeaway. But while there is no greater sound than the Uber Eats guy ringing the doorbell on a Friday night, the truth is this: they don't exactly cook those things with your wellbeing and nutrition in mind! I'm not saying you can never order a pizza again (I'm definitely going to), but what about if, for a change, you challenged yourself to cook your favourite takeaway at home? Cooking a fakeaway is so worth it, but it does take some motivation and you need to go and get all the stuff in. So if you want to plan ahead for Friday, then do that. Whether that's a full Chinese banquet, a pizza wrap or a homemade cheeky Nando's. Or what about learning to make samosas or sushi, if you've never done it? That's an impressive thing to be able to do.

39 How do you really feel?

Check in with yourself. What's your biggest worry right now? What are you most excited about? Don't pretend to yourself that you are fine if you're not. Take a few minutes to yourself and think about what's going on with you right now. If you realize your brain is feeling a bit heavy, reach out to someone to help lighten the load.

40 Drink enough water

Yeah, it's simple but it's still good to remind ourselves about the basics sometimes. It's good for your brain, your skin, your digestive system – everything really. Figure out how many times you will need to refill your glass or water bottle to get over the two-litre mark and consciously count your refills throughout the day. You could draw a smiley face on a Post-it note every time you go to the tap to help you remember.

41   Say thank you

This is an easy one. Think of someone you are grateful to and make sure they know it. It could be your best friend for being lovely or your partner for doing the dishes three nights in a row. Anyone who has helped you with something and/or taken a load off your shoulders. Say thank you and don't forget to tell them why it made a difference to you and how much you appreciate what they do.

42   TWO-WEEK CHECK-IN!

You are halfway through your theme. How's it going? Have you made much time to reflect on it? Today, think about if there is any practical action you'd like to take, if you haven't already. Is there anything you'd like to try out or change?

43 Laugh

Did you know that when we laugh, endorphins are released into our body, making us feel better? And that laughing gives our muscles a workout? But apparently, while children laugh on average about 400 times a day, adults only manage 15. How sad is that?! So your mission today is to laugh as much as you can. And spread the joy around – how many people can you make laugh? Because when someone else laughs, we tend to laugh, too.

44 Buy yourself some flowers

It doesn't have to be anything fancy. Just a small bunch will do. Or bring some in from the garden. Make sure you put them where you see them a lot. Remember, you deserve to have lovely things around you.

45 Eat dinner by candlelight

Whether you're with your partner or your housemates, on your own or with your kids, sit round the table, light some candles and turn off as many lights as you can (definitely no screens at the table!). Yes, they might think you've lost the plot, but doing just one thing a bit differently can change the mood of a whole day. (If you think your family won't get on board, flick the switches in the fuse box and tell them there has been a power cut!)

46 Today, I am grateful for . . .

It's time to take a breath and think about all the positives. What lovely things do you have in your life that you are grateful for? What rocks your world and makes a difference to you? Write them below:

_____

_____

_____

_____

_____

_____

_____

_____

_____

_____

47 Make a playlist

First, pick a theme. Like 'The best songs to listen to first thing in the morning', 'My favourite songs when I was a teenager', or 'Summer's day'. Now build an awesome playlist that you can crank up when you need to put a bit of a spring in your step.

48 Make your water more interesting

How did you go last week on the water challenge? It's true that water is boring and it is easy not to drink enough. So today, change it up a bit by adding something. I like lemon and cucumber slices but you could also try mint, orange, lime, even strawberries. You can also get these orange-flavoured protein sachets which taste good and have virtually no calories. I personally really notice the difference to my skin and hair and to my concentration when I drink enough water, so it's definitely worth finding ways to make it more interesting.

49   Be still for five minutes

Try to find a time today when you can just take five minutes to sit still and do nothing. You can look out of a window or close your eyes (no napping!). Think about whatever you like, but try to keep your thoughts positive or at least neutral. Set an alarm on your phone so you know when then time is over (put your phone out of reach!). This can be surprisingly difficult because we are so used to constant stimulation, but it's a really good thing to try out.

50   Get some film recs

Pick at least five of your friends and send them a message along the lines of: 'What is one of your favourite films that you think I might not have seen?' Make a note on your phone and try to remember to watch them. You might discover something amazing from one of your friend's recommendations or even get a bit of an insight into the things they like . . .

51 Take a 'photo' of something beautiful

Ha ha, not you! (Though you are beautiful, of course!) As you go about your day, I want you to keep a lookout for something that you find unexpectedly pretty and take a photo of it . . . BUT – and here's the twist! – I want you to do it with your MIND! Give yourself a moment to really look and take in the thing that has caught your eye. And, when you get home tonight, try to conjure up that image again and describe it or draw it here. See? We don't need to rely on screens and phone cameras all the time. Our eyes and our brain are pretty cool too.

52 Tell yourself a story

As we know from our vision boards, our imagination is an amazing and powerful thing. Think of something you'd like to happen, even if it feels unlikely. Winning a prize, getting a part in a film, meeting a hero of yours. Whatever you like. Now write about how it happened, as if it really did. Think about the details – who was there, what things looked and felt like, even what you were wearing! Start with the line: 'The most amazing thing happened!' Have fun and try to make it sound as exciting as possible. How we talk to ourselves and the stories we tell are important – so why not enjoy some daydreaming?

_____

_____

_____

_____

_____

_____

_____

53 Choose your own adventure

Today, I want you to come up with something that feels a tiny bit adventurous and plan a time when you can do it. It's doesn't have to be climbing Mount Everest or anything! How about a walk with your partner somewhere neither of you have been before? Or an overnight camping trip with friends or a treasure hunt with the kids? How about an activity you've not tried before or haven't done for ages, like mini golf or a game of tennis?

54 Give someone a gift

It doesn't have to be something you have bought, though it can be. If you have time, you could make a cake for someone. Or if you have really enjoyed a particular book and you know someone who would love it, why not pass it on? Or what about those earrings you never wear but you know your mate loves? It's a lovely feeling to be given something unexpectedly, so put a bit of that energy out into the world.

55 Celebrate!

Happy eight-week bookiversary! How are you feeling today? Let's check in again with all the things that have made you feel happy over the past few weeks as well as thinking about the great things you did, so you can give yourself the pat on the back you deserve. Don't forget – a win is always a win. It's all about what it means to you and not anyone else.

_____

_____

_____

_____

_____

_____

_____

_____

_____

_____

56

Choose your theme #3

It's time to pick another of these for the next four weeks. If you picked something pretty emotional last time, maybe think about something more practical for this one and vice versa.

MY THEME IS

57   Just do you

Here's a challenge for today. I want you to try to consciously notice every time you compare yourself to someone else. Either favourably or unfavourably. So, for example, if you think: *She's fatter than me*, or *He's cleverer than me*, or *At least my car isn't in as much of a state as hers!* We all do it. It's sort of the way humans are made. But it is good to recognize when you are doing it because it's often not helpful, can allow in negativity and wastes energy better spent elsewhere. Once you notice it, you can stop it!

58   Wise words

What is your favourite quote? Is there something you read or heard somewhere that really resonated with you? Write it down below and think about what it means to you and why that particular quote appeals. (You can pick more than one if you want.)

_____

_____

_____

59 Clear some clutter

Most of us will have at least a few spots in the house that are absolute clutter magnets. The corner of the kitchen, a table in the hall, sideboard. Tackling it is a boring job, but it feels so good when it's done. For extra motivation, take a picture before you start and after you finish to show what a difference your ten minutes of work has made!

60 Try a walking meditation

If you're not sure about meditation, then this is a super-easy way to start as you are out doing something rather than sitting still with your eyes closed. You can do this anywhere really. Start by paying attention to your body. How does it feel today? Are your shoulders hunched? Now try to give some attention to how your body moves and your steps (which will feel weird to start with). Count them out 1–2–3–4 if it helps. Bring your attention to your surroundings when you need to (e.g. don't get run over!) but try to remain aware of your movement rather than letting your mind drift off.

61 Have a feel-good movie night

Get the snacks ready, pick a favourite film or one strongly recommended by a friend and settle down by yourself or with some mates. If you need some ideas, here are some of my faves:

- ★ *Pitch Perfect*
- ★ *Maid in Manhattan*
- ★ *The Little Mermaid*
- ★ *Kevin and Perry Go Large*
- ★ *Meet the Fockers*
- ★ *Brave*

62 Detox your social media

Today, I'd love it if you'd spend ten minutes looking at the accounts you follow and checking in with yourself to make sure they all make you feel good. There is enough negativity out there in the world already – you don't need to allow more into your life via your phone screen. If something makes you feel bad for whatever reason, then unfollow. Or mute, at the very least.

63 Buy some fruit

What's your favourite fruit? Treat yourself to a bunch of grapes, a shiny mango or a big slice of watermelon. You'll be surprised how good it makes you feel!

64 Your one simple thing

I always try to make the bed when I get up in the morning. Even if I'm having a bad mental health day, it's the one thing I always try to get myself to do. It's a really important part of my morning routine and I know that I will always feel better if I do it. What's your one simple thing? What do you try to always do because it grounds you or helps you feel ready to face the day? If you do suffer from bad mental health, then maybe you won't manage it every single day, and that's fine. But I think it's good to be consciously aware of these things and what they mean to us.

My one simple thing is: _____

_____

_____

_____

65 Listen #1

Today, try to be really mindful of how you listen to others. Do you cut people off before they have finished their sentences? Are you taking in what they are saying or is your mind elsewhere? Do you respond to what the person is telling you or are you just waiting for your turn to speak?! Yes, it's annoying when your colleague keeps banging on about her holiday or you just need the kids to shut up and put their shoes on, but making the effort to check in and notice when we aren't giving other people our full attention when we should is a good thing to do.

66 No TV night

Yep, you read that right! Step away from the boxset. It'll still be there tomorrow! You can do whatever you like instead – read a book, go out, make out with your partner – but stay away from the screen and give your eyes and brain a break.

67 Have a bath

The tried-and-tested self-care treat! Even if you aren't really a bath kind of person, I'd love it if you gave it a go today. Try to make sure you aren't disturbed. You can listen to music if you like, but sometimes it's nice to just enjoy the quiet.

68 Be your own agony aunt

There's something really therapeutic about writing something down. So often things are clearer when you get them out on the page. Think about a problem you have or a decision you need to make. Write it out as if you are writing to a problem page in a magazine – so not too long! Even writing it can give you some perspective. Leave it at least an hour or so and then come back to it. Pretend you are responding to someone you don't know and see if you can write a reply with some helpful advice.

69 Important/urgent: to-do list

Do you have way too much on your to-do list?
Is it an ever-growing mountain looming over you?
This is one well-known technique for sorting through
the priorities.

★ In the top left box, write the things you have to
  do that will cause a problem if you don't do them
  and have to be done soon (like getting the car
  MOT'd).

★ In the top right-hand box, write the things that
  do have consequences if you don't get them
  done but which aren't so urgent.

★ In the bottom left box, write anything that is
  urgent but less significant (like doing the big
  shop).

★ In the bottom right box, write all the other things
  that don't have a specific deadline and are not
  very important.

How does it feel seeing your to-do list separated
out like this? Can you bin off anything from the 'not
important/not urgent box'? Do you need to set some

reminders for the 'important/not urgent stuff' so you can postpone these things while you get the urgent stuff done but don't forget about them? Can anyone help you with any of this?

	Urgent	Not urgent
Important		
Not important		

70 TWO-WEEK CHECK-IN!

You are halfway through your theme. How's it going? Have you made much time to reflect on it? Today, think about if there is any practical action you'd like to take, if you haven't already. Is there anything you'd like to try out or change?

71 Eat mindfully

Today, instead of bolting down your lunch or grabbing a snack from the fridge without even thinking about it, I'd love it if you'd take a little time to check in and think about what you are eating. Sitting down to eat and chewing properly is so much better for our digestion for a start. Take a moment to consider what you are eating, what it tastes like, why you like it. Try to have a proper meal at a sensible time, rather than eating late or filling up with snacks.

(Note that if you have any issues around food, only do this if it feels good. You are totally fine to skip it.)

72 Moisturize your hands

An easy one today as we all need a day off sometimes! Simply grab some hand cream and take at least a minute to really work it into the skin, cuticles too, and over the wrist. It's easy to spend lots of time (and money!) on products for our face but then completely forget our poor, dry, hardworking hands. Thanks, hands. You're great!

73 Today, I am grateful for . . .

It's time to take a breath and think about all the positives. What lovely things are you grateful for? Write them below:

_____

_____

_____

_____

_____

Our feelings about our bodies are different for each of us and can change by the day. However you feel right now is fine. You are not failing if you don't 'love your curves', or whatever the latest message is. Although I do think we owe it to ourselves to try to block out the negativity we receive without even realizing it. Objectively, your body is great – think of all the stuff it can do. And most importantly – it's YOURS.

74 Look in the mirror

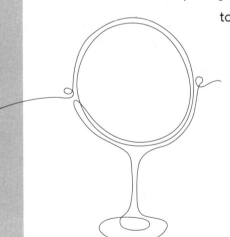

We're going to start strong this week. Today, and every day this week if you can, I'd love it if you would just stand in front of the mirror for a moment without posing, or sucking your tummy in, or turning to a more flattering angle. Try not to think anything negative or even positive about yourself. It's just how you look and it's fine.

75 Pick one thing you like (or are trying to accept)

I really hope there is at least one thing you do like. Maybe you have lovely thick hair, strong arms, a cracking arse. Maybe you're a fan of your ankles or you like your little finger. Try to pick at least one thing and think about what it feels like to be totally at ease with that part of you. If you are still working on trying to accept your body, that's fine too. There's no rush, but you absolutely deserve to get there.

76 Say, 'Thank you, body'

Your body is not an ornament designed for looking at. It's nothing to do with other people. So let's think about what your body *does* rather than looks like. If you've had kids, are pregnant right now or hope to be in the future, that's obviously pretty amazing. Has it allowed you to complete any physical challenges, like half-marathons or going for long hikes? Has it allowed you to travel to cool places in the world, swim in the sea, dance on dancefloors? Take a minute to say a quick, 'Thank you, body. You are amazing.'

77 Let go of all unrealistic expectations

For ages I held on to my size-eight jeans. I could sometimes squeeze into them but they were so tight that my tummy hung over them. I eventually realized that this wasn't because my tummy was too big, it was because *there was not enough space in these tiny jeans!* So why did I keep them? Why did I have this expectation that I would one day magically fit back into them? Even if I did ever fit into those jeans, what would that have achieved? My life would be exactly the same, I'd just be hungrier! We all put unrealistic expectations on ourselves. If you have any, write them down so you can see objectively that they are not helping you. You can then set fire to them if that helps!

78 All bodies are different

We are all built differently! I could eat and exercise the same as you and our bodies would never look the same. Today, make a conscious effort to notice when you are making a judgement about someone else's body or style choices and deliberately find something positive instead. Actors and reality TV stars, models in magazines and quite a lot of social media content don't represent the average body. When criticism of how people look is all around us in the media, it's not surprising we can get judgy, too. But we have to stop! If we stop judging others, we learn to be less critical of ourselves too.

79 Challenge opinions

How many of your decisions about what you wear are influenced by other people's opinions? We all love positive feedback and if you always get compliments on a particular dress, then it's nice to know other people like it. But ultimately, real confidence comes from within. If you are relying on approval from others, that is not confidence. I know I feel better in myself when I have my hair up and I'm in my sweats, even though I get more compliments when I wear a dress and have my hair loose (though getting compliments is lovely and I do appreciate them!). Today, think about the things you like about your body, your clothes, your hair, and check in with yourself to make sure this is really *your* opinion.

80 Positive affirmations

Welcome to the last day of body confidence week. How have you found it? I don't know how you feel about affirmations. The point of them here is to train your brain to see and say nice things to you, which then teaches your eyes to notice each good thing. If you're into affirmations and mantras, then go for it – you'll know what to do. If not, how about we start with some promises to our body, to try and improve the relationship we have with it? Here are some ideas for promises to make to your body. You can also come up with your own.

★ I promise not to be rude or nasty to you any more.

★ I'll treat you with love as far as I am able.

★ I won't listen to what random people say about you, or what I am imagining they are saying about you.

★ I'll remind myself to nourish you with healthy food and lots of water.

★ I promise to remember how important good sleep is.

★ I promise to try to keep you strong by being active whenever I can.

81 Give yourself a face massage

The best time to do this is when you are putting your face cream on in the morning or at night. Or you can use a facial oil.

- ★ Start on the side of your face and neck, running the flats of your fingers down the sides towards your chest.

- ★ Put your thumbs together under your chin and push them along the underside of your jawbone towards your ears.

- ★ Now use your fingers in a circular motion on your cheeks, lifting them as you go.

- ★ Use your first two fingers to massage small circles all around your mouth.

- ★ Finally, using your middle fingers, start at your chin and push them up either side of your nose, and onto your forehead

Don't worry too much about the exact technique – focus on what feels good to you. The point is to relax those muscles and get the blood flowing.

82 Important/urgent: self-care

So, you remember two weeks back, you filled in the 'important/urgent' grid with things from your to-do list? Well, we're going to do the same thing again but this time with the things you do that matter most.

- ★ In the top left box, write the things that are important to you and which you have to do soon or regularly to help you feel good (e.g. 'I need to run every couple of days'; 'I really need a holiday'; 'I get lonely when I don't see my friends regularly'). Anything where you'd feel crap quite quickly if you didn't do them.

- ★ In the top right box, add the things that matter to you but that you don't need to do all the time (e.g. a night out with the girls every couple of months, an upcycling project).

- ★ In the bottom left, write down the things you spend some of your free time regularly doing that you like but you wouldn't notice if you didn't do them for a while.

- ★ In the bottom right box, put the things you sometimes do in your free time but you could happily live without.

	Urgent	Not urgent
Important		
Not important		

83 Important/urgent: self-care review

Today, let's look back at that grid you filled in yesterday and ask some questions.

★ Do you think your priorities here actually reflect how you live and spend your time? For example, if it's important to you that you and your partner have a date night once a week or fortnightly, do you make the time to do that?

★ What about the things you spend your time doing regularly but actually aren't that important to you. Could you sack that off sometimes to make room for the things you care about more? For example, if you didn't spend so much time watching reality TV shows, would you have more time for a favourite hobby?

★ If you do stuff occasionally and don't really care about it, do you need to do it at all? Like, if you sometimes go to a pub quiz with your partner but don't enjoy it, would they be just as happy to go with a mate instead?

It's important to remember that you don't need to be super-productive all the time. It's FINE to lay about on the sofa and watch *Come Dine with Me* if that's what you feel like. This is just a way of checking in, of reminding yourself what you really care about so you can make sure you get to do the things that matter to you as much as possible.

84

Celebrate!

Twelve weeks of *One Win a Day!* Tomorrow, you'll be choosing your new theme for the next four weeks, but first, how have the last four been for you? What have you enjoyed this month? What have you felt good about? Ticked anything off the to-do list? Write them down here.

_____

_____

_____

_____

_____

_____

_____

85

Choose your theme #4

What's it going to be this time? If you picked something pretty emotional last time, maybe think about something more practical for this one and vice versa.

MY THEME IS

86 Get rid of clothes that don't fit you

This is sort of a follow-up from body confidence week. If you haven't already, your challenge today is to get rid of any clothes that don't fit you. Honestly, you don't need to see them all the time and your wardrobe will feel less cluttered if you get them out of the way. If you really think there is a chance you will want them again, then you can box them up and put them somewhere, but do ask yourself if you really will.

87 Sit up straight!

Yes, I know I sound like your mum, but honestly, good posture is so important. It opens up the chest so you can breathe better. It protects your spine, engages your core and it makes you feel more present. So no curling up like a woodlouse, let's take up some space, yes? Today, try to be really conscious of how you sit and to catch yourself when you're slouching – you could even set a reminder on your phone to catch you out!

88 The best advice I've ever been given . . .

Today, ask as many people as you can what the best piece of advice they have ever been given is. Write the best ones here – the most interesting, that strike a chord with you or are just really funny. (My favourite? 'Don't eat yellow snow'!)

_____

_____

89 The 'I actually don't give a shit' card

My gift to you today is one (and only one!) 'I actually don't give a shit' card. Use this at any point in the day when you are supposed to do something you really don't care about. Obviously, some basic, sensible rules apply: there shouldn't be any serious consequences and I expect you to always give a shit about your health and wellbeing. But do you know what? If you don't want to wash up before you go to bed tonight, then don't. If you're not up for your colleague's birthday drinks, don't go. Play the card and give yourself a break.

90 Learn the name of a tree

I don't mean like 'Alun the tree', I obviously mean the type of tree! I bet there's a tree in your garden or outside your house that you have no idea what it is. Take the time to go look at the leaves and the bark and then Google around until you find out what it is. We can take nature for granted, but it is such a healing thing in times of stress and anxiety, and learning the name of a plant or flower is one way to slow down and connect.

91 Clean your shoes

Some of you will probably be rolling your eyes at this because it's not the most exciting job in the world, but I think it's worth doing for at least two reasons. One, because getting these small, everyday tasks out of the way can be very satisfying. A quick win, basically. Also, shoes are expensive, and so getting the mud off them, cleaning trainers so they are white again and polishing the ones that need it means they will last longer and look nicer. Did you know you can put Crocs in the washing machine? They come out looking brand new!

92 Make one thing better about your everyday routine

Think about your normal day. Getting up, getting to work or the kids off to school, your commute . . . Walk it through in your head and think about if there are any simple changes you could try to make your day just a little bit nicer. If you are always in a rush in the morning, would getting out your clothes the night before help? Do you need a Thermos mug so you can take your coffee with you in the car? Or perhaps doing a bigger food shop at the weekend would make dinner times easier in the week? You deserve a life that's as stress-free as possible, so start with something small and see how it works for you.

93 Harness Parkinson's law

Parkinson's law is that a task grows in size to fill the time given to it. So if you could easily get ready in twenty minutes, but you have thirty minutes before you need to leave, then that's how long you'll spend. Or, if you have two weeks before some work is due, you'll spend longer doing it than if it was due in five days. Sometimes, there's a way to use this to get boring stuff done. If you think you can get some housework done in the half-hour before you have to go out, put it in that slot so you can't take more time over it. It's a good feeling to use deadlines to your advantage and feel like you're in control of them.

94 Today, I am grateful for . . .

It's time to take a breath and think about all the positives. What lovely things are you grateful for? Particularly focus on the small things that just make you happy. Write them below:

_____

_____

_____

_____

_____

_____

95 Draw your own coat of arms!

You know how in the olden days, noble families and knights would have a family crest? Well, today, I want you to draw one of your very own! What are the things that are most important to you? What sums up who you are and what you love? Pick four of them and find a way to represent them in the four sections below (it doesn't matter if it's a bit abstract!). Now see if you can come up with your very own motto and write it underneath . . .

96 Know you are great

How are you at accepting compliments? This is good for everyone, but especially if you are one of those people who's all like, 'No, I'm not, stop it!' when someone says something nice. Think about any compliments you've received recently. Anything. 'Cool shoes!', 'That's a good idea', and even people asking for your advice are all compliments. If you can't think of any, that's probably because you brush off nice things people say as it makes you uncomfortable. Try to take it in when someone compliments you in future and simply say, 'Thank you'! Over the next two or three days, write down any compliments you get here:

_____

_____

_____

_____

_____

_____

97 Compliment three people

So yesterday you thought about compliments that you have received. Today, it's your turn to give out some appreciation. It can be for anything, but the key is you have to mean it! Think about what those around you are really good at and tell them that they are awesome.

98 TWO-WEEK CHECK-IN!

You are halfway through your theme. How's it going? Have you made much time to reflect on it? Today, think about if there is any practical action you'd like to take, if you haven't already. Is there anything you'd like to try out or change?

99 Plant love

Get yourself a cloth and a bowl of water. Walk around the house and gently dust off the leaves of all your house plants until they are clean and shiny. (Wash any trays that have got a bit grubby while you're at it.) All living things need care. Taking a moment to nurture the plants is a good reminder to take time to nurture you, too.

Wardrobe TLC

So now you've got rid of the clothes that don't fit you (see Day 86), you might have a little more space and be able to see the wood for the trees. Is there anything in your wardrobe you like but you don't wear because it needs fixing? Maybe a hem has come down on a dress or you have a pair of jeans that are comfy but finish in a weird place on your leg and would look better cropped? If you don't feel confident with a needle and thread, do you know anyone who might be able to help? Perhaps you could do a skill swap if there is something you are good at that they need help with? Failing that, simple repairs and alterations can be done at the dry cleaner's for not much money. It's much better for your bank balance and the environment to fix something you have than to go shopping.

101 Find the things that inspire you

If you're a visual person like I am, I think you will enjoy this. Gather some photos and pictures that make you feel creative, inspired and/or positive and put together a collage somewhere you'll see it – like on the wall next to your desk, on the fridge. You might want to include photos of people you love, fantasy holiday destinations, places you have actually been, favourite song lyrics . . . Anything that makes you feel strong and inspires you to live the kind of life you want to live.

102 Try a new craft

You don't have to go out and buy a pottery wheel or anything – just pick something simple and give it a go or make a plan for the weekend. There are so many crafting videos online it's ridiculous. Knitting, origami, upcycling, embroidery, collaging . . . Trying to learn to do something new like this is good for the brain and it can be a good way to press pause on whirling or anxious thoughts.

103 Forward fold

If you've ever done Pilates, you'll know this one. It's sometimes called a roll-down. Stand with your feet apart the same width as your shoulders, feet facing forwards. Keep your legs straight but knees relaxed. Take a deep breath in. Slowly drop your chin down to your chest and then start to roll down towards the floor – imagine the bones in your back starting to curl forwards one at a time, your arms just hanging in front of you. Gently breathe out as you're doing this. Get your hands as close as you can to the floor without it hurting and keeping your legs straight.

Hang there for a moment and then take another breath in before doing the whole thing in reverse, a vertebra at a time, until you're back upright again, exhaling the whole time. This is so good to decompress the spine, improve mobility and give everything a bit of a stretch – especially if you work at a desk all day and even if you don't.

(If you have back issues, though, skip this one or talk to a qualified Pilates or yoga teacher first.)

VISION BOARD!
Fun with friends

What would your perfect weekend with your friends look like? Daydream about some amazing things that would be perfect for your gang. Get dressed up and go to a fancy restaurant? Go camping and drink red wine around a fire? Get your mates involved, if you like. Write or sketch about it in the box below. Some might be total fantasy, but is there anything here you *could* do?

105 Get all your account numbers in one place

You'll need to think carefully where to store this, but it can be so useful to have all your account numbers for utilities and things like that saved in one place. Take half an hour today to do this bit of life admin, and it will save you time in the future as you won't need to hunt through paperwork every time you have to speak to your internet provider.

106 Sell something you don't use any more

You cleared out your wardrobe on Day 86. Now, what do you have in your home or garage that you're not using? Would someone else want it? See if you can get a few quid for it from selling it online – for example, on eBay or Facebook Marketplace. Someone else might be really glad of it and you will free up space in your house.

107 Plant a seed

Whether it's some cress on your windowsill or something more ambitious like an acorn, it's lovely to watch a little bit of nature sprouting under your very eyes. How much success you have will depend on the time of year, among other things, but have a go. It's sort of like life. Not everything you plant is guaranteed to grow and flourish, but if you don't try you'll never know.

108 Organize some photos

Most of us take a lot of photos but then they just sit on our phones. If you have ten minutes to kill today – like on the train or when you're waiting for the oven to heat up – scroll through, find some of your favourites and put them in an album. This could be of your best friends, your family or maybe some of the best times you've had recently. It's lovely to have them all in one place to look over if you feel a bit down.

(109) Shelf love

Take a look at your bathroom shelves or dressing table, wherever you stash make-up, hair stuff, toiletries. Now gather together anything that is obviously out of date and congealing, or anything that you tried but didn't work for you. If you're not sure if something is out of date, check the back. There will be a symbol that looks like a jar with the lid off and a number next to it. That tells you how long the manufacturer expects the product to stay effective after it's been opened. It's up to you if you want to keep using it after that – you just might want to keep this in mind with things like suncream, where if they don't work it's a problem. Chuck out anything that is unusable and you'll be amazed how much better you feel.

110 Find a comedy podcast

Remember a couple of months ago when you had a day when you tried to laugh more? Here's an easy way. Put your favourite comedians' names into a podcast app and bookmark or download some episodes. You'll have a ready-made playlist for your commute/cleaning the bathroom/whenever you need a distraction from something boring.

111 Celebrate!

That's another four weeks gone since we last did this! It's time again to grab five minutes and celebrate the wins, the wows and the wonderful things! Take a moment to reflect on what you've accomplished over these weeks.

_____

_____

_____

_____

_____

Choose your theme #5

How are you finding your themes of the month? Are they easy to choose? It's fine to make them specific if there's something you really want to give a lot of your energy to – like decorate the kitchen or pass your driving test – but don't be afraid to choose something more abstract sometimes too. You might want to think about what happiness means to you or how you can get in touch with your creative side.

MY THEME IS

113 Make it fun

What's your least favourite chore or task? What do you always put off doing because you find it so boring or annoying? Let's find a way to bring in some fun today. Can you use the podcasts you downloaded on Day 110 to listen to while you're doing it? If you have to go somewhere to do it (like going to get the car washed), can you tie in a visit to your favourite shop or bakery on the way home? If you know there's something good in it for you, you'll be less likely to put it off.

114 Walk somewhere you'd usually drive

Is there somewhere you could walk to even though you usually drive or get the bus or the train there? If you can't walk all the way to work, how about getting off the bus a stop or two early? If you can, pick a favourite upbeat album to listen to on your journey and think about your theme of the month.

**Start your new habit
and give yourself a
gold star every day
you do it.**

115 · One good habit

Studies have shown that it takes around sixty days to form a new habit – when you just start doing something automatically and don't have to think about it any more. What habit would you like to have? Pick something simple – like always putting your keys in the same place when you come in, taking healthy snacks to work – and think about how you can incorporate this into your routine so it feels easy. Start your new habit and give yourself a big fat tick or gold star every day you do it. And who knows, once you've shown yourself you can do it, you might find that other habits you want in your life are easier to form.

116 · Look at some cool art

You don't have to travel to a big city to look at paintings or photography – you can do virtual tours online of lots of the most famous galleries. Even if you think art isn't really your thing, take a few minutes today to try to find something that interests you. What is it about that painting, photo or sculpture that appeals to you? Does it make you feel a certain way? You could search for local artists too, to find out what people are creating near where you live.

117 Your very own cheer squad

You know in American films when the football team scores and the cheerleaders wave their pompoms and start doing acrobatics? Today, I want you to imagine you have your very own cheer squad who are rooting for you and celebrating your every tiny win. What colours do you want their uniforms to be? Think about them jumping up and down when you have sent a well-written email or forming a human pyramid because you remembered to buy milk before it ran out! GO YOU!

118 Watch something inspirational

Reality TV and detective shows where people keep getting murdered can be good escapist telly, but I don't think many people would say they are inspirational! It's always a good idea to look for positivity where you can find it, so look for a documentary about someone who did something incredible or beat the odds and watch that tonight instead.

119 Set the table

Rather than just grabbing a fork off the draining board and digging into your dinner sat on the sofa, make an effort to lay the table properly this evening with cutlery, water glasses, napkins if you have them, etc. It will only take a couple of minutes to make it look nice. You can do it just for you or get those you live with to join you. Phones away, obviously.

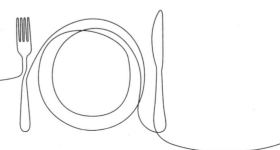

120 Have a social-media-free day

I LOVE social media, but I do have to take a break sometimes. We can get sucked in and sometimes feel we are living our lives through our phones. If you think it's going to be tough, you can remove the app icons from your phone screen temporarily so you don't open them without thinking. They won't be deleted, just not right there calling out to you!

121 Do some moon-watching

The moon was sacred to lots of ancient cultures and some people today believe it's an important feminine symbol. Whether you're into that idea or it's a bit too New Agey for you, I think we can all agree that a big full moon looks cool. Google the lunar cycle and figure out whether it's a waxing (getting bigger) or waning (getting smaller) moon at the moment. Make a note in your diary when the next full moon and new moon are going to be, and try to remember to look out for it. It's a way of counting the passage of time that we don't think too much about any more and might just give you a different perspective.

122 Your favourite wins

OH MY GOD, we are a third of the way through our 365 wins already! Today, I'd love it if you would flick back through the book and think about what your favourite wins were. What did you really enjoy doing? (Did you remember to colour in the stars in the corners of the pages?) Write your favourite ones below:

123 Your least favourite wins

While I hope you've had fun over the last four months, there were probably some challenges I set that you've loved less. Perhaps you just don't care that much about flowers or it turned out that your friends have terrible taste in films! But were there any you found particularly hard? Does this teach you anything about yourself and what you are comfortable with? Remember, there is no such thing as failure here. The thing is to learn more about ourselves and what makes us tick. Not everything in life is easy and if it gives us the opportunity to reflect and maybe even grow a little, then that's a definite win.

124 Plan some nice breakfasts

I think that even if you are not really a breakfast person you could give this a go this week, as it is good to change up your usual routine and start the day with something nice. If you usually just grab a bowl of cereal, think about what you'd enjoy instead. You probably don't want anything too elaborate, but what about some muesli, fruit and yogurt? Or bagels or crumpets for a change? If you really don't think this is going to work for you, then at least plan some nice breakfasts for the weekend and make time to go to the shop so you've got stuff in to make it with.

125 Exfoliate

Our skin is constantly shedding dead skin cells and if these hang about they clog pores and make skin look kind of dull and sad. If you have time today, have a soak in the bath and then use a mitt or a scrub to get rid of them. If you're short of time, have a quick scrub with a mitt in the shower (but doing it in the bath and seeing the grey ring left behind is both satisfying and gross!).

(126) TWO-WEEK CHECK-IN!

You are halfway through your latest theme. How's it going? Have you made much time to reflect on it? Today, think about if there is any practical action you'd like to take, if you haven't already. Have you thought of anything you'd like to try out or change?

(127) The comfort bank

This is a little bit like the happiness bank we did way back on Day 34. Below, write a list of the TV shows, books, films, music or activities that you find reassuring. The things you know you can fall back on when you are tired or stressed because they are easy and comforting. Fold the corner of this page or colour in the star so you can find it when you need a reminder.

128 Kitchen disco

What music always gets you dancing? While you're making the tea tonight, crank up your favourite artists or find an awesome playlist online and dance your heart out. Sing along too – spatulas, wooden spoons and whisks all make great microphones.

129 Call a friend

You might talk to your friends all the time on Messenger or WhatsApp, but how often do you speak to them on the phone? Think of someone whose voice you'd love to hear and pick up the phone. It's lovely to make the time to do this with friends who live a long way away. You could message them in advance and ask when they are free so you know you're calling at a good time, if that makes you feel more comfortable.

130 Make a cleaning schedule

If you love cleaning like I do, you're going to enjoy this. If you hate it you won't, but I still reckon you'll find it really useful! Make a list of all the jobs you have to keep on top of to keep your home the way you like it. Divide the list into three parts – jobs that need doing more than once a week, roughly once a week and every two weeks or less often. Then, order those lists by how long each chore takes. You could put them in three sections again: jobs that take ten minutes or less, those that take around twenty minutes and those that are longer. This is not only really handy to refer to if you feel like the housework is getting out of hand, you also can use it as a prompt or a reminder. So if you have ten minutes free and you fancy getting something done, you can scan your ten-minute section and decide what's the priority.

131 Today, I am grateful for . . .

It's time to take a breath and think about all the positives. What lovely things are you grateful for right now? Write them below:

_____

_____

_____

_____

_____

132 Go outside for no particular reason

Go on. Go and stand in the garden or walk round the block. Take some deep breaths and try to clear your mind. You aren't going anywhere or doing anything. Take in the fresh air and just *be* for a minute.

VISION BOARD!

Perfect Sunday

What would your best ever Sunday look like? What time would you get up, what would you do, who would you spend it with? Doodle, draw or write your ideas below. Let your imagination run wild, but when you've finished, have a think as to whether you could actually do any of these things this weekend, or next month. How much thought do you give your Sunday plans on a normal week? (Or whatever the equivalent of Sunday is for you, if you work weekends.)

134   Review the happiness bank

One hundred whole days ago now, on Day 34, you started your own happiness bank, full of things that usually work to cheer you up if your mood is down. Flick back to that page now and have a look. Have you used the happiness bank? Did it help? Is there anything you want to add to it?

135   Unsubscribe from emails

It's unbelievable how cluttered your inbox can get when pretty much every online company signs you up to their mailing list (unless you get your magnifying glass out to find the tiny box you have to tick to opt out). It means you get a lot of general junk. And if you get loads of emails headed 'FLASH SALE! DON'T MISS OUT!' it can make you feel like you need stuff you don't, or you waste time scrolling through a website only to realize you don't want anything and it's only tiny discounts anyway. So take some time today to find that unsubscribe link at the bottom of marketing emails and reduce your amount of junk.

136 What else could you 'unsubscribe' from?

I think there's a life version of being sent unwanted marketing emails. Sort of like finding you are signed up to something you didn't ask for. That might be a friend who always complains about stuff in their life without ever asking you how you are, or maybe a task at home or work that *always* seems to be your job even though other people should be contributing. Are you experiencing this at the moment? Think about anything that's draining your energy and consider if there is a polite and reasonable way you can 'unsubscribe' from it.

137 Cold-water therapy (part one!)

If you've never done it, then it might sound crazy, but I promise you'll get used to it and it's the most invigorating way to start a day. It's just a small thing but I find it so good for my mental health. If you're new to it, just turn the shower to cold right at the end and see if you can stand there for thirty seconds or a minute to start with.

138 Make a playlist for someone else

Is there someone in your life who's going through a tough time and might need a pick-me-up? Or who has mentioned they are a bit stuck in a rut with their music and would love to have something new to listen to? Make a playlist and send it to them.

139 Celebrate!

We are now twenty whole weeks into *One Win a Day*. Before you write down your favourite wins and best moment of the past four weeks, why not take a quick moment to flick back over the previous 'Celebrate!' entries (you'll find them at numbers 27, 55, 84 and 111) and take a minute to think about all the great things you are doing *all the time*!

_____

_____

_____

_____

_____

140

Choose your theme #6

Theme SIX already! What's been your favourite one so far? Ideally, I'd like you not to repeat any just yet, but if you found picking something in particular as a theme really helped you, then you could always choose something else in a similar area for this month, and build on what you focused on before.

MY THEME IS

141 Use your mind to cut someone down to size . . .

Most of us have someone in our lives who we feel intimated by or who puts us down. It's often a boss or someone at work but it might also be a family member. Take a minute to imagine them sitting on a chair and getting tinier and tinier, until their silly little legs hardly reach the end of the seat. Now imagine them getting really frustrated, their face turning purple because they're having a tantrum about being stuck in the chair. They don't seem so intimidating now, right? Remember this image next time you have to deal with them!

142 Learn a new word

A silly one, a useful one or an obscure one – you choose! Try to use it three times today so it sticks in your head – and because it will be funny to try to shoehorn it into conversations!

143 Change something about your appearance

Just something simple. For example, do your hair a different way, change up your accessories or try out something new with your make-up. We are always changing and evolving as people and this can mean the way we like to dress too. This is a good way to remind yourself to dress for you and try to have fun if you can. It doesn't matter what anyone else thinks.

144 Do a puzzle

It could be a crossword, a sudoku, a jigsaw . . . whatever you like. Challenge your brain while soothing it by taking fifteen minutes out to concentrate on something away from your day-to-day worries and to-do list.

(145) Revisit a childhood obsession

What were you really into when you were a kid? Were you fascinated by space? Did you collect Pokémon or love horses? Whatever it was, give yourself ten minutes to Google the subject now. Can you find any posters or toys you used to own online? Remind yourself of what you used to know about your favourite subject and what it was like to be a little kid who doesn't care about being cool and just loved whatever grabbed their imagination. I think we could all do with a bit more of that in our lives . . .

I get asked a lot by my followers about confidence. You might categorize yourself as a confident or unconfident person, but for everyone, there will be some areas where you feel you really know what you're doing and some where you feel really unsure. So this week, let's focus on where you're at with your self-confidence, and what you can do about it . . .

146 How confident are you?

Let's start by thinking about what confidence means to you. It's also important to try not to compare how you feel on the inside to how other people seem on the outside. Just because you know a woman who looks like she always knows exactly what she's doing, it doesn't mean she's not bricking it on the inside sometimes!

I feel most confident in situations when

_____

_____

I feel least confident in situations when

_____

_____

147 Where does your confidence come from?

Today, let's focus on the situations where you do feel confident. I love to do karaoke and I know that I have a good voice for it. I feel confident getting up in front of people to sing because I have done it lots of times (doing things over and over helps with confidence). I've always had loads of fun, so I associate it with positive memories and people have said nice things about the way I sing.

What do you feel confident doing? It doesn't have to be something in front of people – like karaoke or public speaking – maybe you're really good at maths and you feel confident when you are faced with a page full of numbers (OMG – lucky you!). Take a minute to think how this feels and where that confidence comes from.

(148) What if you weren't afraid?

Is there anything that you would like to try that you haven't because it feels outside your comfort zone? Anything at all. Asking someone out, speaking up at a meeting, starting a new hobby, joining a group . . . Make a note of any time you think a lack of confidence might be holding you back.

(149) When did you work through the fear?

I bet there have been times when you had to do something that you would have much rather not. When you had to be brave and just get on with it, even though you didn't feel at all confident. Try to think of three times when you were worried about something but it was all OK in the end. Maybe not brilliant – though if it was then that's amazing! – but none of your worst nightmares about what could have gone wrong happened. Is there anything to be learned from those experiences?

150 Say yes and step outside your comfort zone

I was staying somewhere for work once and there was no room service. So if I wanted to eat dinner (which I definitely did!), I had to go down to the restaurant and sit by myself. I really didn't want to – I'd never eaten in a restaurant on my own before and I thought people would stare. Of course, no one did! I doubt anyone even noticed. Sometimes, if we're going to get out of our comfort zone we need a push. Have a think today about what you can say yes to that feels a bit challenging. If you put yourself in a position when you just have to do something, so often you will find that you can do it, that your confidence was there all along. I promise you that you are capable of SO MUCH!

151 Talk to someone

As ever, talking to the right person about how you feel can be a key that unlocks a door. Either because once you hear yourself say the problem out loud, you realize it's not actually as big or complicated as it was when it just lived inside your head, or because the other person shares your worry or has been through something similar. It's a great way to put worries aside and build confidence. Also, if you want to start going to a class or group, you could always see if anyone you know wants to go with you . . .

152 No one cares what you do (in a good way!)

I hope you've found it helpful to think about confidence, and you've found it to be a positive thing to do. The main thing to remember is that you don't have to be the most confident person in the room. You're not failing if you feel unsure sometimes – we all do! Often the loudest person in the room isn't actually the most confident. You don't need to be 100 per cent sure about something to give it a go. Most of the time, no one else will even notice if you try something and it doesn't go well. Everyone is too busy worrying about their own stuff! End this week by making a commitment to just having a go. What's the worst that can happen?

(153) How good are you at being by yourself?

I just want you to check in with yourself today and decide how much you like to do things by yourself. Are you someone who is happy to go for a coffee alone and you like having the freedom to do that? Or do you prefer to always be with someone? I think it's good to be aware of this, and doing things alone that we'd usually do with a partner or friends is one way to grow confidence. But we are all different and have different comfort boundaries and that's OK too.

(154) TWO-WEEK CHECK-IN!

You are halfway through your theme. How's it going? Have you made much time to reflect on it? Today, think about if there is any practical action you'd like to take, if you haven't already. Is there anything you'd like to try out or change?

155 Notice kindness

Today you don't exactly have to do anything, just be extra aware of what's going on around you. There's so much in the news about people being horrible to each other that we can forget that, actually, most people are decent and doing their best. So today, your job is to spot any act of kindness going on around you, no matter how small or ordinary. Like a kindness I-Spy.

156 Find a new restaurant or café

Maybe it's for a potential meal out this month, or perhaps you want to research a special treat for an upcoming event. Spend fifteen minutes or so having a wander around the internet and see what you can find. Has anything opened recently in your local area? It's fun to have ideas stored away in the back of your mind for future date nights or meals with mates.

157 Make the algorithm work for you

Social media algorithms get a lot of bad press, but basically they just want to know what you want to see. This does mean that if you look at content that maybe isn't great for your mental health, then it's probably going to serve you up more of the same. But you can counter this by deliberately searching for hashtags of things that you find uplifting and inspiring. This will up your chances of being followed around the internet by things you like. (It's also an incentive not to give in to clickbait links as you are telling the internet that this is what you want!)

158 Inspire yourself!

When you have a few spare minutes today, rather than scrolling, start a folder of photos of things from your own life that inspire you. This could be beautiful views and sunsets you've seen to remind you to get outdoors more. Or if you're a brilliant baker you might create a folder so all those gorgeous cakes are in one place and you can scroll through and admire your own genius. Maybe you need a folder of pictures of you with your best mates to remind you how many people love you and have your back. We can go on Pinterest for inspiration of course – I do all the time to get ideas for upcycling projects or decoration. But I bet there's some stuff in your life already that's pretty cool and could inspire you.

159 Move some things around in your house

I'm all about mixing things up from time to time so you don't get stuck in a rut. One way to do this is to change your physical environment. Have a look at your furniture, the way your stuff is arranged. Could any of it be moved around? What would your bedroom or living room be like if some of the furniture was in different places? Or what about the way you store your clothes in your drawers and wardrobe. Is there another way of doing this that might work better? You might end up putting it all back again, it's true, but who knows what you might discover and how it might change your perspective?

160 Learn a card game

While I think it would be cool to be a poker player, like in the movies, realistically I don't have the patience (or any interest in gambling!). But I do think it's great to have a card game to bust out. We love playing Rummi and Switch in our house.

161 Download an audio book

Whether you're a big reader or not, it's always nice when someone tells you a story. There are lots available online for free and you can also sign up to a free trial for the main providers. (Just remember to put a note in your calendar to remind you when it expires so you don't get charged if you don't want to use the service any more!)

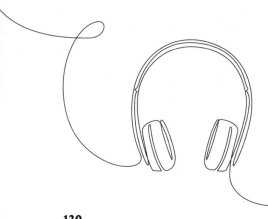

162 Look at a cloud

I love looking at the sky. Today, take a moment to pop out and just give your attention to the big old expanse of sky above your head. If it's summer and you can, lie on the grass in the garden or a park. Pick a cloud and watch it move across the sky for a minute. Think about how some problems can seem big or overwhelming but then they pass and don't seem so huge after all. Most things do pass.

163 Audit your sleep routine

Sleep is so important to our bodies and our brains – not least our metabolism, memory and mental health. And if you are sleep deprived it has a knock-on effect on so many things. So today, think about how a good night's sleep feels to you. Is there anything you can do to get in the right headspace before bed? For lots of us this will be staying away from screens before bedtime, but if you give it some thought you might decide some new bedding or pillows is a good idea, for example, or making sure you don't eat dinner too late.

Most things
do pass

(164) Change your phone screen photo

Change up your phone screen today. Be intentional. What would you like to see every day? Is there something you put in your inspirational folder last week? Or maybe you'd like to choose something that ties into your theme of the month?

(165) Be still for ten minutes

Remember back in week seven when I challenged you to sit still for five minutes? Now let's see if you can manage it for ten! Again, you can look out of a window or close your eyes (still no napping!). Think about whatever you like, but try to keep your thoughts positive, or at least neutral. Notice what you are thinking about. Set an alarm on your phone so you know when the time is up, but put your phone out of reach! How did it feel? Scary? Relaxing? Does it feel strange to just be still with your thoughts for a while?

(166) Nostalgia trip

What was your favourite book, TV show or film when you were a kid? Can you remember what it was that made you love it so much? Share your memories with a childhood friend or sibling who liked it, too. Even if you end up shouting lines from *Friends* or *Harry Potter* at each other, it will be a fun trip down memory lane!

(167) Celebrate!

Guys, it's that time again! It's not cheating if you want to write things down throughout the month, by the way. If something cool happens and you want to make sure you remember, then you have my permission to skip ahead to the next Celebrate! and put it in so you don't forget.

_____

_____

_____

_____

_____

168

Choose your theme #7

Ready for this? What are you going to choose as your theme this time? If you need some inspiration, think forward to some things you are going to be doing. If you're going on holiday, maybe the theme is relaxation (and how you can do more of it!). If it's back-to-school time for the kids, maybe you could think about learning new things too . . .

MY THEME IS

_____

169 Today, I am grateful for . . .

It's time to take a breath and think about all the positives. What lovely things are you grateful for? Write them below:

_____

_____

_____

_____

_____

_____

170 Make your gratitude list visual!

How have you been finding making a gratitude list? Is it helping you to remember all the things – big and small – that have gone well and you're happy about? Today, let's reflect even more and make it visual! Take or find some pictures and create a folder on your phone of some of the things you are most grateful for.

171 Troubleshoot

Like I always say, as you can't wave a magic wand and fix the big things, sorting out those that it is in your power to fix is the next best thing! Today, think of something small and recurring that annoys you or holds you up. Like, 'I can never find my keys', 'I often forget to take my lunch to work', 'I can never remember my password'. What simple thing can you try to get rid of that irritation from your life? How can you make sure you always put your keys in the same spot? How can you remind yourself to get your lunch out of the fridge? What can you change your password to that's memorable?

172 Tell someone they are amazing

Here's a simple thing most of us don't do enough – simply send someone you know a message to tell them why you think they are amazing. Or a reason you admire them. We think good thoughts all the time about our loved ones, but how often do we *tell* them?

173 Easy-win savings

Today involves a quick bank account audit, so if you are really struggling financially at the moment and can't face looking at a bank statement, you have my permission to skip this. Think back to your favourite win in the book so far and do that again instead. For everyone else, log on to your online banking and have a scroll through the last month, asking yourself the following questions:

★ Are there any direct debits here for subscriptions I hardly use?

★ What small things do I spend money on often and how much do I value them?

★ Are there any regular outgoings that are for things I don't need and that don't enhance my life in any way?

If, for example, you only had one TV subscription service running at a time rather than three and you decided to take a coffee to work just one day a week instead of always buying one, you're probably going to be saving around £20 a month. What could you spend that money on instead? That face cream you really want but feels a bit too expensive? How long would it take before it adds up to the cost of the jeans you want?

174 Wear something colourful

There's something really fun about wearing bright colours. So today, grab some of your brightest things out of the wardrobe and go the full children's TV presenter if you want to! If you're someone who wears a lot of black this might feel weird, but give it a go as far as you are comfortable. Don't worry what anyone else thinks – in fact, if anyone comments that what you are wearing is quite bright, then mission accomplished! Give yourself a gold star.

175 Get your screen time down

Do you get a notification every week telling you how much time you've spent on your phone? If not, you can find out in the 'settings' section of most phones. Are you happy with this number? If you'd like to spend less time on your phone, why not set a target? You may also be able to set up your phone to mute notifications at certain times of the day and limit time for apps. This can help if you find yourself mindlessly scrolling when you don't want to.

176 Make some morning time

This might not sound like the most exciting thing to start with, but bear with! Before you go to bed tonight, think about what you can do to make the morning easier for Tomorrow You. So, put out your clothes for the morning. Make the kids'/your lunch and put it in the fridge. Get everything you need ready to go as much as you can. Then, in the morning, use that extra time you'd usually spend rushing around to do something for you. If it's just an extra fifteen minutes in bed, that's fine! Or maybe you'd like to read on the sofa before work, meditate or go and grab yourself a fancy coffee. Whatever you like – this is quite literally your time.

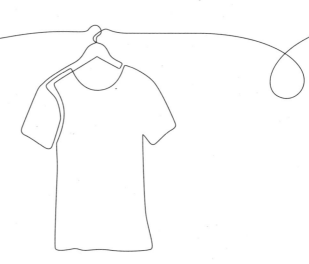

177

VISION BOARD!

A room in the house

One of my favourite things to do! If you could change one room in your house, and money was no object, what would you do? Sketch or write some ideas below. If you are considering doing some decorating, come back to this vision board at a later date and think how you could make some of your dreams a reality. As someone who once turned a wreck of a house into a cosy little home with hardly any money at all, I can promise you that there are so many ways of doing this that don't cost the earth.

178 Write a funny poem – for yourself or someone you love

Hopefully all that colour the other day has put you in a good and possibly silly mood! I think there's something really refreshing about just being a bit silly. So today, write a funny poem (rhyming or not, up to you) for someone you love. Maybe a message for your kids or your best friend to tell them you love them in a funny way? Or just to tell your partner to pick up some bread, but in the form of a silly poem?!

179 Watch a gig on YouTube

If you don't have much time to see live music, there isn't a lot going on near you or big crowds aren't your thing, this is a fun alterative. Find an artist you like and see if they have put any of their live gigs on YouTube. If you want to, you can turn down the lights in the living room, put your drink in a plastic cup and have a dance, just like you are there (but much nearer your own toilet!).

(180) Three things I learned today

Our brains are amazing things. We are constantly picking up new bits of information, solving problems and finding things in the depths of our memory banks. But we can take this for granted. At the end of the day, try to come up with three things you learned today. They don't have to be clever or life changing. Just three things you found out today that you didn't know yesterday.

1 _____

_____

_____

2 _____

_____

_____

3 _____

_____

_____

181 Get steamy

Give yourself a salon treatment at home. Steaming your face opens up your pores, which can release trapped sebum and bacteria and increase the circulation in your face. It feels relaxing too. If you have eczema or any similar skin condition, then you might want to give it a miss, though.

Simply get a big bowl of very hot water (so it steams, obviously!) and a towel. Take your make-up off and clean your face. Put your face over the bowl and the towel over your head to keep the steam in. Don't put your face too close to the water, take a breather if you need to, and if it feels like your skin is burning – stop! Some people like to add essential oils to the water – this is great for relaxation and if you have sinus issues. Just don't go too nuts as it might irritate your skin. Five to ten minutes will be enough. If you moisturize or use serum after steaming, your pores should still be more open and absorb the products better.

(182) TWO-WEEK CHECK-IN!

You are halfway through your theme. How's it going? Have you been able to reflect on it? Today, think about if there is any practical action you'd like to take, if you haven't already. Is there anything you'd like to try out or change?

(183) Go to the cinema on your own

My partner H loves going to the cinema, but to be honest this isn't something I really do. But if I was away for work and had a free evening, for example, I think I absolutely would. I mean, if nothing else you don't have to share your popcorn and can eat as many snacks as you like, right?! If you do want to feel more confident going to things by yourself, I do think you could consider doing this. It's a really easy place to start as you're there to watch the film and it doesn't really matter if you know the person sitting next to you, does it?

Self-care Bingo

I love a game of bingo, me! Now that we're halfway through, which of these wins do you want to make into a habit? Add them into the bingo card below, and make a promise to yourself that you'll do everything to get a full house over the coming weeks!

			Go outside first thing
	Buy yourself some flowers		
		What are your superpowers?	
Make a cleaning schedule			

185 Buy a new pen

There are fewer reasons to write things down now than there used to be, as so much is on our phones. But, as I really hope you've found over the last six months (!) working your way through this book, it can be quite soothing to slow down and write – in your own unique handwriting – rather than type. So, today, consider treating yourself to a new pen to encourage you to keep up the habit. It doesn't have to be fancy, but a bit more than a Bic biro, ideally! Something you will enjoy using.

186 Important/urgent: self-care review . . . review!

On Day 83 (all those weeks ago!), I asked you to look at your self-care important/urgent boxes and see if there were any changes you wanted to make. So how did you get on? Don't worry if you didn't make any changes – change is hard! But now is the time to go back, have another look and see if you feel inspired to try to do anything differently.

187 | What makes you move?

If you're already motivated to play sport or work out, this probably is less of an issue for you. But for many of us, when we feel tired or hormonal or low we can get out of the habit of just getting up and moving. Even when that would realistically be quite a good thing to be doing. So, kind of like when you made a list of all the nutritious food you actually enjoy, I'd like you to make a list below of all the active things you like doing to remind you when you are feeling stuck to the sofa or unmotivated. They don't have to be organized sports or anything. Kitchen discos are totally valid. As is walking the dog and pushing the vacuum cleaner around while listening to loud music!

188 Give yourself a deadline

Tough love today, guys! Pick something on your to-do list that's been sitting there for a while. Set a deadline. How are you going to hit that deadline? What do you need? Put it in your diary or find another way to remind yourself. Importantly, how are you going to reward yourself when you get it done? Now imagine how good that's going to feel!

189 Invent a mocktail

There are so many alcohol-free drinks on the market now, so feel free to have a look at those for inspiration. But I'd like you to have a go at creating one of your very own – your signature mocktail! You can make it cool and classic or chuck a load of pineapple and cocktail umbrellas in. Up to you!

190 Plan a booze-free Friday

OK, now you have your mocktail sorted, how about planning a booze-free Friday? If you don't drink, maybe this will be a sugar-free Friday. It's not about booze or sugar being really bad (you'll have your own opinion on this), it's more about teaching our brains that we don't always have to have a massive glass of wine or a load of ice cream to mark the end of the week. What could you do instead that you would look forward to all week? What could you replace these things with that would still feel exciting or like a treat?

191 Worry list

What are the first four things that come to mind if I ask what is worrying you right now? If you want to, write them down here. But if you don't want to record them in the book, use another piece of paper. Then you can bin it or ceremonially rip it to shreds!

_____

_____

_____

_____

_____

_____

_____

For each, ask:

- ★ Can I do anything to resolve the problem or make me feel better now?

- ★ Are any of them completely outside my control?

- ★ Is there someone I can talk to about any of these?

If you answered no to the question above – are you sure? Even if it's just to vent or say how you feel out loud?

I'm not saying that asking these questions is going to stop you feeling worried, but it's sometimes good to examine the things that are bothering us and ask if there is anything we can do, rather than just letting the bad thoughts fester.

Finally, if you had to take one off the list – if I said narrow it down to three – which would you remove? Can you park that for the moment and deal with it another day? Not always possible, I know, but if you get overwhelmed, small worries can grow out of all proportion in your head.

192 Main-character energy

What would your character traits be if you were the lead character in a book or film? What is your story? What challenges are you facing right now and how could your story unfold? You are still you in this game – not a millionaire or randomly a famous TV presenter! – but you can pretend you are the author of your story and write about what comes next from the moment you are in right now until . . . whenever you like.

193 Research a trip

Do you have any trips or holidays coming up? Even if it's just an idea at the moment, or something you've been saying to your girlfriends that you must do but there's no date planned yet, take fifteen minutes to learn a bit more about your potential destination. What are the top things to do? Can you find a cool-looking restaurant in your price bracket? Which might be the best neighbourhood for you to stay in? Not only is it fun to imagine yourself away somewhere, you'll be much more likely to go once you've found out more about it.

(194) Screen time check-in

It's been three weeks since you looked at your weekly screen time. Did you set a goal for this? If so, how have you got on? If the answer is, 'Not well, in truth, Charl!', then don't worry, let's take a moment to figure out why and what might be getting in your way. What are you spending the most time on? You can usually see which apps you are using the most. What would be the easiest thing for you to cut back on?

(195) Celebrate!

Pens and wins at the ready! What were your favourite things over the previous four weeks? Don't forget to pat yourself on the back for anything you achieved that felt good to you. It doesn't matter what anyone else would think about it; you are the only judge here.

_____

_____

_____

_____

_____

196

Choose your theme #8

It's time to pick another theme. What are you going to focus on and make an effort to think about over the next four weeks? Imagine it like this if it helps: if your life was a garden, which bit might need a little more water?

MY THEME IS

197 Sock drawer audit

Just like we did with knickers, it's time to sort out the sock drawer. And I'm including tights here too. Get rid of anything with holes or that's not really wearable any more. Any single socks that lost the other half of their pair (where do they GO?!) should be binned, too, if you're not going to wear them. There's no point having a tangle of useless socks and tights. They are only going to get in the way and make it harder to find things and get dressed in the morning.

198 Send some compliments

According to some people, what we put out into the universe is what we get back, and I think I buy into that. We did this on Day 97, but you need to get into the habit! So today, send out some good vibes by complimenting people. Maybe on social media or a message to a friend. For example, 'Thanks so much for dinner last night – you are an amazing cook!' Don't forget – you have to mean it or it doesn't work. (And try to not make it about you. For example, 'I wish I was as good at cooking as you are!' is putting yourself down, whereas this is about you simply telling people who are great that you appreciate them.)

(199) Cold-water therapy (part two!)

So it's been a while since I asked you to try to this out. How do you feel about having another go? Maybe you've gotten really into it or perhaps you are groaning out loud! But sometimes we have to try things more than once and let ourselves get used to new experiences and sensations. So if you can, turn the shower to cold again today and see if you can last a little longer. Admit it, it wakes you up at least, right?!

(200) You are STILL great!

And while we are on the subject of trying things more than once – how did you get on with thinking about how good you are at accepting compliments and not brushing them off? Today, let's repeat the exercise. Write down the compliments you get today here. Again, some compliments are subtle – they can come in the form of a thank you or someone valuing your opinion, for example.

_____

_____

_____

Being kind to ourselves is such an important part of good mental health. And taking the time to spread a little kindness makes the world a better place. So that's what we're going to do this week!

201 Kindness makes the world go round

Today, I just want to start with something simple. Really make the effort to say thank you and to acknowledge every good thing that someone does for you. Whether it's a stranger holding a door, your colleague making you a cup of tea or your kids getting on with something they'd usually complain about. Let's be grateful for the small things as well as the big things, and show that we are.

202 Thank yourself!

Today, I want you to say thank you to yourself. You might feel a bit silly at first, but go with me on this! Every time you do something that is helpful or kind to you and your sense of wellbeing, acknowledge it by saying: 'Thank you, me!' For example:

★ Choosing the healthier lunch rather than the plate of carbs you know will put you into a coma in the afternoon.

★ Getting your clothes out the night before so you feel less rushed in the morning.

★ Getting a boring task done rather than putting it off.

★ Doing some exercise even though you fancy slumping on the sofa.

203 Listen #2

Do you remember waaaay back on Day 65 when I asked you to think about your listening style? Today, let's be more specific and consider how we respond when someone is telling us about a problem they are having. It's so tempting to jump in and offer solutions and advice. Particularly if it's someone younger than you or who you feel responsible for. It's completely understandable if we feel like we want to 'fix it'. But so often, what that person needs most, or at least first, is for someone to listen to them.

★ Can you show that you are listening and trying to understand what they are saying?

★ Can you find a way to acknowledge what they are feeling?

★ Can you ask them questions (sensitive ones!) to try to help them figure it out for themselves rather than going straight to: 'Well, what I think you should do is . . .'?

★ Take a moment to think about how they might experience things differently from you, and that their reactions and ways of coping are different.

(204) Ask someone about their passion

Do you know what the people around you are really into? What hobbies or interests make them tick? Today, try to find out a bit more. We all love to talk about the things we like to do. You might discover a whole new side to someone, or at the very least learn about something you had no clue about before!

(205) Buy flowers for someone else

When you bought yourself some flowers back on Day 44, and popped them on your desk or windowsill, was it nice to have something cheerful to look at? Today, if you can, why not do that for someone else? It doesn't have to be a massive bouquet, just a little bunch of tulips from the supermarket is fine! Who do you think would really appreciate this?

206 Make time for someone

Sometimes the very best gift we can give anyone is our time and attention. Today's challenge is a bit of a general one, so the first thing you will need to think about is how to make it specific to you and someone in your life.

Who might appreciate you taking some time for them? Is it someone junior at work who has been struggling and might appreciate you offering to talk them through some task they're finding hard? Is it a friend who's going through a tough time and would like to go for a walk with you and talk it through? Maybe you've not seen your mum or dad for a while and they would love to go for a meal with you or pop round to yours one afternoon?

It's OK if you offer and someone doesn't respond the way you thought they would. There could be so many reasons that are nothing to do with you. The point is that you try. Because that's all any of us can do.

207 Cut the negative self-talk

Let's finish kindness week by checking in again and making sure you are being kind to yourself. If kindness is all about treating others as we would want to be treated, then that means we have to be nice to ourselves first and foremost, right? So try to catch yourself every time you say something mean about yourself in your head. Notice it and actively think: *No, that's not nice. I deserve better than that.*

I know this is going to be harder for some people than others. At the very least, when you catch yourself being negative, follow it up by saying to yourself: 'But you're still amazing!' If you're struggling right now you might not believe it straight away, but I promise it's a really helpful habit to get into. You have the power to change your thoughts!

208 Today, I am grateful for . . .

It seems like a good idea to follow up kindness week by reflecting on some things we are grateful for. Write them here:

_____

_____

_____

209 Film night

How long do you think you spend scrolling through Netflix or whatever trying to find something to watch? If you're like me, maybe as long as it takes to watch something! (There's too much choice! And why are there so many films about Christmas?!) Today, start a list of all the films you've always meant to watch or that have been recommended to you. Did you watch all the recommendations you got from your friends back on Day 50 yet? If you make a note on your phone, you can add to it whenever something else springs to mind and you'll have a ready-made film and TV show menu at your fingertips.

210 TWO-WEEK CHECK-IN!

You are halfway through your theme. How's it going? Have you made much time to reflect on it? Today, think about if there is any practical action you'd like to take, if you haven't already. Is there anything you'd like to try out or change?

211 Practise calm – the 5-4-3-2-1 technique

This is an exercise that is sometimes recommended if you have anxiety, so you might be familiar with it. It might work for you, it might not, but I always think it's worth trying these things so you have something you can turn to if you start to feel overwhelmed.

★ Sit quietly and focus on your breathing. Try to take slow, deep breaths.

★ Look for five things you can **see** around you – any individual things in your surroundings.

★ What four things can you **touch**? Your hair, maybe, the seat you are sitting on, the carpet under your feet . . .

* Now listen. What three things can you **hear**? Try to identify something far away and something close to you, even if it's your own breathing.

* What two things can you **smell**? If there's something near by like soap or some clean laundry, then pick that up and give it a sniff!

* What can you **taste**? What's the last thing you ate? Can you still taste it in your mouth?

How did that feel for you?

212 Make a playlist for your gang

Ready for another playlist? How about making a playlist for your group – or your family if that's what you want to do. What are the songs you have in common? Was there a gig you all went to, a band you all liked when you were at school? You can start it off and then make it collaborative, so everyone can add songs that remind them of others in the group.

213 Good habit #2

Three months ago now (I know! Time flies!), you had a go at introducing a new habit you wanted in your life. How did it go? If you're still keeping it up, then that's brilliant and I'm really proud of you! If not – that's OK. Why do you think it didn't stick? Was it too unrealistic for your life right now? Or perhaps you took the wrong approach and need to try doing something differently. If you're raring to go and want to start introducing another new habit, then go for it. If you want to try again with the last one, that's fine too. You might just need to be a bit more honest with yourself about what works for you and why – and let's face it, we should all be trying to be as honest with ourselves as we can.

214

VISION BOARD!
Dream job

Let's get our imaginations going again! If you could do ANYTHING, what would it be? Get specific – where are you doing this job, what are your surroundings? What is a typical day like? Do you have co-workers, a team? What are they like? Draw or describe it in the box below.

215 Reasons I like my job

We are all so quick to moan about work! We don't want to go to work, we complain about it when we're there and we can't wait to leave work, only to hit traffic – then do it all over again the next day! So today, why not break that cycle and write down some reasons why you actually like your job? There will probably be some things you jot down here that you wouldn't think of day to day. But even if your job is just a job for you or you're going through a bad patch with it at the moment, I think there is probably something you like about it. Whether that's the people, helping customers, or even just nicking stuff out of the stationery cupboard! Write down the reasons below to remind you not to lose sight of the good bits.

216 Declutter your workspace

While we're on the topic of work, take time today to have a sort of your workspace. Whatever you do and wherever you work, I reckon you can find a way to make things a bit cleaner and tidier. When you're busy and stressed, the last thing you need is stuff all over everywhere getting in your way, so take a moment to get organized.

217 Upcycle

If you know me, you'll already know that I bloody love an upcycling project. Taking something ugly or boring, coming up with an idea for it and making it match the vision in my head is so satisfying. Today, think about how you might change something in your house. A plant pot, an ugly lamp, a side table . . . Choose something realistic for how much time you're going to have in the next few weeks and how much effort you want to put into it. Do some research on Pinterest to get ideas and to figure out what materials and techniques you're going to need.

218 Have a fancy coffee

Today, find time to treat yourself to a nice coffee, or a tea, or a hot chocolate with all the bits, or even a smoothie if that's what you fancy. Ideally, this would be made by someone else, not you. When you have it in your hand, try to take a moment to really enjoy it. Remind yourself that you deserve nice things. They don't need to be big or expensive, just good things for you to enjoy as part of your day.

219 Beat the clock

I hope this won't sound stressful – it's supposed to be a fun challenge! Allocate slots for your tasks today, setting times for how long you think each task will take. So you might think: *I'm going to try to finish this work call by 12.30, this piece of work by about 1 p.m. and then go for a walk in the sunshine. Or, I'll have dinner at seven and these are the things I want to do before bed, which I'll do at this time, leaving me this amount of time to relax.* I'm not saying do this every day, of course, but it can be interesting to consciously know how long things take you. And putting tasks into slots can stop them mushrooming and then your whole evening being taken up by one thing.

**Remind yourself
that you deserve
nice things**

220 Check the lighting in your house

It might seem like a tiny thing, but how your lights are positioned in your home can make a big difference to how it feels, especially in the winter months when you need to have the lights on more. Harsh or bright overhead light can feel draining, and too dim light not only makes it hard to see what you are doing, it can make you feel sleepy too! Tonight, have a walk round your house, asking yourself:

★ Do the lamps all have the right bulbs in them for their size and where they are?

★ Are all the lamps in the right place? Are there any dark corners that could do with some more light?

★ If you have any spotlights that move, are they pointing the right way? E.g. to your kitchen bench so you can see what you are cooking!

★ Are you happy with the lightbulbs in your overhead lights? Are they warm or cool, and are they bright enough?

You can always move some lamps around temporarily to get a sense of whether it will make any difference to how a room feels and then rearrange all the plugs, etc. to make it permanent once you're happy your idea will work.

221 Your happy place

Where is your favourite place in all the world? Somewhere that brings back happy memories or that you love to go back to. Perhaps it's your very own garden on a summer's day. When you have a quiet moment today, think about that place and try to walk around it in your imagination. How does it make you feel to do this? Find some pictures if you need to. If you don't do this already, would it help to imagine yourself there when you feel stressed or anxious?

222 What's your favourite word?

Something silly or inspirational? A person's name (your dog's name?) or something completely nonsense? My favourite word is 'lush'. It's a proper Welsh word for 'nice' and I use it all the time – it's literally lush! Play a game and see how many times you can use your favourite word today . . .

223 Celebrate!

It's time to give yourself a pat on the back again!
Think about all the great things that have happened
over the previous four weeks. All wins are wins.
Anything that has made you feel happy is just as
valid as everything else.

_____

_____

_____

_____

_____

_____

_____

_____

_____

224

Choose your theme #9

What would you like to give some thought to over the next four weeks? It doesn't have to be very specific – perhaps there's just a general area of life or the kernel of an idea bubbling away at the back of your brain that you want to give some space to . . .

MY THEME IS

225   Free writing

Today, I'd like you to spend five minutes free writing. This means you just write, for a set period of time, about whatever comes into your mind. Try not to pause, grammar or even sense don't matter, and don't read anything back until the end. It's just about letting words flow completely uncensored from your brain to the page. If you need a starting point, you could use your theme of the month and see where it takes you.

226   Change up something in your home

Do you have a sideboard, a mantelpiece or some shelves where you display things? Today, change it around a little. Do you have any beautiful things hidden away in drawers that you'd like to put out? How about incorporating something to remind you of the season – like a vase of flowers from the garden or autumn leaves? If you have photos in frames, it's nice to rearrange these sometimes as you will start to notice them again when they are in a different spot where you're not used to seeing them.

227 Do something good for the planet

What can you do today to be a slightly better citizen of the planet? Have a think about your average day and how you might be able to make small changes to be more eco-friendly. Try finding ways to use up all of your leftovers and avoid food waste. Are there some journeys you could make on foot rather than jumping in the car? There are plenty of resources online to help you research your options, and some changes may save you money too.

228 Leave a good review

Online reviews are increasingly important for businesses. If you had a brilliant experience at a local business, say thank you by making time to leave a review on TripAdvisor, Google or somewhere similar. Or, how about sending positive feedback about a particular person? For example, if the receptionist at your doctor's is always really kind and helpful, can you send a quick email to the practice to say how much you appreciated their help? You might just make someone's day.

229 | Pick a mantra

A mantra is a word, a phrase or just a sound said over and over to help with focus in meditation. Mantras come from religious and spiritual practices and go back over 3,000 years. 'What does this have to do with me?' you might be asking. Well, you can use the idea of a mantra – a short phrase you repeat to yourself – in your day-to-day life to help you feel more focused and confident. Even if it sounds a bit too woo-woo for you, give it a go. First, you need to come up with one, based on what feels right for you today. Most start with 'my' or 'I' and are short and sweet. They should only contain positive words. For example, 'I choose to feel calm.' 'I deserve to be loved.' 'I am happy with the person I am today.' Repeat your mantra to yourself throughout the day, especially if you feel stressed or overwhelmed.

230 | Keep an open mind . . .

Colleen Hoover once said, 'Keep an open mind; it's the only way new things can get in' and it's really stuck with me! Just remember everyone you meet knows something you don't, so make a commitment today to be a little more open-minded and willing to learn from others!

(231) . . . and challenge your assumptions

The problem with human brains is that while they are amazing, they make a lot of assumptions and like things to be simple. Have you heard of 'confirmation bias'? This is when our brains look for information that fits in with things we already believe and ignore stuff that might contradict it. It's not our fault; it's mainly just our wiring. The best way to correct this is to consciously look for reasons you might be wrong, rather than reasons you are right. It's fine to get things wrong. What's not OK is to be so afraid of being wrong you close your mind to learning about other people and refuse to change your opinion. Today, try to catch yourself making assumptions about things, events, people. Check out your logic or your reasoning, and notice if you need to challenge your beliefs.

232   Set a health goal

It's really important not to take our beautiful bodies for granted and to remember to thank them for all the things they allow us to do (like we did in body confidence week). Is there anything you think your body needs from you right now? Do you think you'd feel better if you got more sleep, ate more veg or made an effort to move more? Today, think about whether you want to set a simple health goal and what that might be. You can even make 'healthy habits' or similar your next theme if you want to.

233   Find Your Scent

What do you absolutely love the smell of? It might be a particular perfume, and that's fine, but is there something in nature that you love, too? Like orange blossom, cut grass, the smell of the sea on holiday? My favourite scent ever is Jo Malone's Nectarine Blossom & Honey. If you're not sure, ask the people around you what their favourite smells are to see if their answers inspire you to decide on your favourite scent.

234 Breathe in

Now you have thought a bit about what your favourite scents are, can you treat yourself to something today that just smells amazing? A hand cream, a scented candle, an essential oil would all work. Even a fabric softener would be a great way to bring that smell into your home, if you can find one that smells good!

235 Batch cook

When will you next have some time to cook? Maybe you could even make extra of whatever you're having tonight and freeze that. It's so great to have some homemade pasta sauce or chilli con carne in the freezer for those days when you really can't be bothered, and so much more satisfying than a ready meal. You could even plan the next few nights' meals based on what leftover will freeze well. Just remember to label them properly, obviously!

236 Good memories

Today, find some photos from a time when you were really happy. A brilliant holiday, a party, a time when you were first with your partner . . . Think about sharing a couple of the photos with someone who was there and sharing memories. Try to remember a detail of that time or that day you haven't thought about for a while and see if the other person who was there can remember anything you have forgotten.

237 Try out the Pomodoro Technique

Have you ever tried this? The idea is that you set a timer for twenty-five minutes and try to concentrate on your work until it goes off. Then you have a five-minute break (you can get up and wander around if that helps) and then you do it again. If you do three or four twenty-five-minute/five-minute break sessions in a row, take a fifteen-minute break. People who find they are easily distracted or who get sucked into a task and carry on even when they aren't actually achieving anything might find it particularly helpful. Give it a try today and see how you get on.

(238) TWO-WEEK CHECK-IN!

You are halfway through your theme. How's it going? Have you been able to reflect on it? Today, think about if there is any practical action you'd like to take, if you haven't already. Is there anything you'd like to try out or change?

(239) Do a facemask

Hopefully giving yourself a few minutes to wake up and check in with yourself has made you feel at least a tiny bit more relaxed today. So why not finish the day with a relaxing treat too and give yourself a facemask? If you don't want to buy one, you could always make one – there are loads of recipes online. While it's on your face, try not to do anything else. Just lie back and relax for the time it takes, either letting your mind wander or you could think about your current theme.

240 Engage with your local community

I'm not suggesting you should run for the local council or anything, unless that's your thing, but it's good to have some sort of connection to what's going on around you. Today, think about how many people you know on your street and how aware you are of things going on and issues affecting your town. Are there any local Facebook groups you could join? How about simply reading the local paper?

241 Your five favourite stories

This could be books or films, whatever you like. But when I say 'favourite' here, I mean the ones you love the most. Not ones you think are cool or are smart and critically acclaimed. Why do these stories mean so much to you, do you think? If they are things you first saw or read when you were young, do you think you learned anything from these stories, or they shaped who you are in any small way?

242　Stressbusting

If I ask you what one thing is making you feel the most stressed at this moment in time, what would you say? Now ask yourself:

★ Is this something I will care about in six months' time?

★ Will I care in one month?

★ Will I care next week?

★ Is there anything I can do now, today, that will make it feel less overwhelming?

★ Is it possible to break it down into smaller parts that don't feel all-consuming?

★ What would I advise someone else to do if they were stressed about a similar thing?

★ What is stressing about this doing to me? Is it helping in any way?

★ Can I ask someone for help?

As with the worry list, this isn't going to magically make the stress go away, but taking a moment to look at it calmly and ask some questions may help you decide what to do about it.

243 Do a different kind of exercise

Some people make exercise seem way more complicated than it needs to be. Really, all we need to do is remember to move our beautiful bodies in a way that's fun – because that is good for our bodies *and* our brains. Today, if you can, try a different kind of moving from what you usually do. It can be anything – find a yoga video online, play Just Dance, go for a swim, have a game of football with the kids in the park or just nick their skipping rope . . .

244 Fix something in your house

I bet there's something that has been bothering you. A squeaky door? A loose handle? A grubby mark on an otherwise clean wall? Take five minutes today to get out the WD40, a screwdriver, the sugar soap – whatever you need – and get that irritating little issue sorted!

245 Make up a game

We used to do this all the time when we were kids, but how often do we do it now?! Today, try to come up with a game. It can be as mad or silly as you like, involve lots of people or just you. Don't make it complicated – just have some fun and let yourself play! I used to love playing The Floor is Lava when I was a kid, and even now I can make it from the sofa to the chair without touching the floor!

246 Do something seasonal

Connecting to the time of year is another way of stopping that feeling of getting stuck in the everyday while time rushes by. It's nice to get out and feel a sense of where you are in the year. What's going on at the moment? Is it pumpkins and autumn woodland walks? Easter egg hunts and cherry blossom spotting? Try to find somewhere to visit or an event going on near you that ties into the season.

(247) Still got it!

What did you used to be brilliant at as a kid? Today is the day to find out if you can still hula hoop, name all the dinosaurs, do the macarena . . . Even better – challenge a friend or sibling who was into similar stuff to you. Send them a picture or a quiz!

(248) Moisturize your body

Take a few minutes today to moisturize your skin. Try not to do it in a rush. Say 'thank you, muscles' for all of the great things they let you do and, if you want to, think about the promise you made to your body in body confidence week, all the way back at Day 80.

249 Power pose

Here's one that might make you laugh! It sounds mad, but researchers have found that deliberately making your body language assertive can make you feel more confident. Try standing with your feet apart, hands on hips and chin slightly up – this is called the 'Wonder Woman pose' (I love it). Take a few deep breaths and remind yourself how awesome and strong you are. How do you feel now?!

250 Get out of your bubble

We get to the point where we know what we like and we tend to look for similar things to watch or listen to and follow lots of the same sorts of people online. Think about how you can change it up a bit. Look for a social media account to follow that's dissimilar to the content you usually see, or read a real-life story about someone who has had a completely different experience to anything that has happened to you. The internet is such an amazing tool for letting us learn about and connect with people who are completely different to us.

(251) Celebrate!

How have the past four weeks been for you? What are you proud of? What has felt good for you? Did you make any progress with your theme of the month? You know what to do!

_____

_____

_____

_____

_____

_____

_____

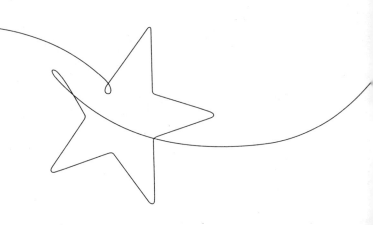

252

Choose your theme #10

It's time to pick another theme. You can return to something you chose earlier in the book if you like, or perhaps something along the same lines? What theme have you felt was the most useful for you so far?

MY THEME IS

253 Health goal check-in

Three weeks ago, you set a health goal – one simple
thing that you wanted to improve to look after
yourself a little bit better. How has that gone for you?
If it really helped, then that's great, well done! If not,
well, you can't win them all. That's just life. But think
about why you didn't. Is there anything standing in
your way to making that small change and can you
can do anything about it?

254 Watch a documentary

Have a scroll through your streaming service,
Google 'best documentaries' or ask friends for
recommendations. What would you like to know
more about? Maybe you'll be inspired by a real-life
story, learn about a bit of history you had no clue
about, or feel relaxed after watching a doc about
whales or penguins . . .

VISION BOARD! Style

Today, I'd love it if you made a vision board that was all about your own personal style. What are the clothes that make you feel good? This isn't about current trends or even what other people have commented suits you – really think about how you dress for *you*. Take some pictures of your favourite clothes that you own or find some photos of you wearing your best outfits and use those as a starting point, rather than celebrities or models.

256 Today, I am grateful for . . .

It's time to take a breath and think about all the positives. What lovely things are you grateful for? Write them below:

_____

_____

_____

_____

_____

_____

257 Book club

Sort of like we did with film night a couple of months back, make a list on your phone or in your notebook of some of the books you've been meaning to read or listen to, to remind you the next time you fancy picking up a book. You could message your friends and ask them what their favourites are.

258 Be positive about something negative!

Oh my god, I cannot WAIT to go to the dentist! It's going to be AMAZING! How we think about things and talk to ourselves is such a powerful thing. Today, see if you can use the power of positive talk to help get you through a task or experience you really don't like. Even if you know you are joking and there's very little you're going to love about it, saying some positive things out loud might genuinely help. Even if you are mainly focusing on how great you will feel when it's done!

259 Learn to recognize a constellation

Not Orion, everyone knows that one! Find out what is visible at the time of year from the place you are now (there are lots of apps that can help you) and next time there is a clear night, go outside and look for it.

260 Encourage nature

What can you do to help nature today? If you have a garden or a balcony, can you get a birdfeeder or birdbath? It's so cool to watch the birds hopping about outside your window. Maybe you have a patch of ground where you can sow some wildflower seeds or you can make a bug hotel?

261 Tell yourself the truth about something

We all do it. We all tell ourselves stories or little porkies about why we do things or we haven't done things. I'm terrible at walking the dogs regularly, and even writing it now, the guilt's hit me like a ton of bricks! I convince myself it's because I'm busy, but I'm just being lazy! Sometimes it's because the real reason feels a bit uncomfortable or it doesn't fit with how we like to see ourselves. But we are strong and we can handle a bit of truth-telling. Plus, it's actually really freeing to admit things to yourself. We are all a bit selfish, a bit disorganized, a bit lazy sometimes. It doesn't make you a bad person! But if you can face up to it, you can move on. Don't let shame or denial get in the way of being the amazing person you are.

262 Remove distractions

Something a bit less heavy today! Our phones are distracting enough without them constantly trying to get our attention, pinging away to tell us about stuff we're not bothered about. So I'd like you to go into 'notifications' in the settings of your phone and check that only the app notifications you actually want appear on your phone lock screen – and only really important, time-sensitive stuff is allowed to make a noise. If you're not sure, turn some off completely for a few days and see if you actually miss anything. As much as I love it, we have to remember that social media and apps more generally are deliberately designed by clever people to keep us glued to them for as long as possible. But we are in charge of our mental health and our time, so we need to make sure we have some healthy boundaries in place.

263 People-watch

When you are out and about today, try to remember to pay attention to what other people are doing. What is their body language? How are they interacting with other people? It's a good way to get you out of your own head and can make you more empathetic.

264 Make bread

You don't have to do this tonight if you are very busy, but think about when you might be able to fit it in. Not all bread takes ages to make. Have a look at recipes for soda bread, parathas or cornbread. Homemade focaccia straight out of the oven is amazing. Or, if you have time, just do a simple white loaf. There's something cool about making such a staple food as bread in your own kitchen. You know exactly what's in it and your house will smell amazing while you make it!

265 Play with bubbles

If you have some kids of your own or some you can borrow, they will love this! Because for little kids what's better than the magic of blowing bubbles?! When we are grown-ups, we can forget about the wonder and fun we used to get from simple things. Which is the reason for today's challenge. And why I want you to get some bubbles and play, even if there are no children there at all!

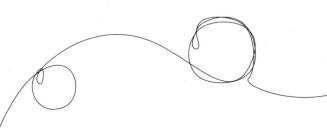

266 Change something in your house that bugs you

When you're at home today, have a wander around your house and find one thing that annoys you. Maybe a scuffed wall, an ugly hand towel you've never liked, a tatty cushion cover . . . Make a plan to sort this out. Honestly, no one really lives in those immaculate, completely styled rooms you see on Pinterest and Insta. They are shot so you don't see the mess in the opposite corner! If there are some things you don't like about your home, then changing them a bit at a time is a definite win. If, however, you don't give a rat's arse that there's a stain on the rug and the curtains are a bit loud, then great. Leave it all exactly as it is. It's your home, so the only thing that matters is how you feel.

267 TWO-WEEK CHECK-IN!

You are halfway through your theme. How's it going? Have you been able to reflect on it? Today, think about if there is any practical action you'd like to take, if you haven't already. Is there anything you'd like to try out or change?

268 Check out events near you . . .

Check the listings in your area for the next month. Are there any bands playing you want to see? What's showing at the cinema? Particularly check out local museums and art galleries that are free – if there is an exhibition going on, then why not pop in? If it's not for you, then you've not lost anything but you might learn something or discover something cool. Write them down to remind yourself and really try to do three of them.

269 . . . and try going to something on your own!

Those things you found yesterday that are happening in your area – would you consider going to any by yourself? Obviously it's great to grab opportunities to see friends, but I do think it's cool to have the confidence to go along to things by yourself sometimes. Plus it can be easier than trying to find a date and time when various people are all going to be free. Sure, some people seem to have been born with the confidence to go anywhere and do anything. But for most of us that only comes from having a go, trying it out and seeing how you feel.

270 Buy Nothing Day preparation

Tomorrow, if it is at all possible, I would like you to spend no money at all. Of course, I understand that you might need to get to work or something like that. But the general idea is to avoid it as much as you can. So have a think about how you are going to do that. If you usually buy your lunch, can you make it tonight and take it? What other things do you spend money on over the course of the day?

271 Buy Nothing Day

My challenge to you today is not only to avoid spending money, but not to engage at all with any kind of retail if there is a way to avoid it. That means no online browsing and no going into a physical shop, even to look. As far as you can (it's hard), try not to look at the ads you get served online and on social media. At the end of the day, ask yourself how that felt. Was it hard or easy? Did it make you question how you spend a few quid here and there without even realizing? Obviously, businesses want to make it as easy as possible for us to spend our cash, so it is good to be mindful of this and make sure the things we buy we actually need or really love.

272 Draw a picture

It doesn't matter if you haven't done any drawing since school (when your art teacher thought your sketch of a dog was a shoe), this is such a good way to relax your brain for a minute. Pick an object near by or a view out of the window and just draw. Don't worry about the finished thing, just focus on the lines of things you can see and how you want to put them down on the page. You can throw the picture away when you're finished, or stick it on the fridge – or submit it for the Turner Prize! Whatever you want.

273 Go somewhere that makes you feel calm today

If you're a book person, maybe browsing the titles in your local bookshop is a happy place. If you love plants, could you stop off at the garden centre on the way home or even just take a slow walk around your garden? Maybe it's your favourite homeware store that makes you feel calm. You don't have to buy anything, just take ten minutes to look at some lovely things.

274 Get a different perspective

Can you work somewhere different? Eat your lunch in a café or park you've never been to? Or just sit and read in a different room? Today is all about literally looking at things from a different angle!

275 Go stargazing

Which constellation did you learn nearly three weeks back? Can you still remember it?! Hopefully tonight will be lovely and clear and you can find a time to go out and look at the night sky. If not, you might have to make a note and set an intention to do it next time there is an opportunity. (You could always watch a video about astronomy and what is visible from where you are in the meantime!) A starry night is so amazing, but in our day-to-day lives, unless we're away on holiday or camping, not many of us take the time to go outside and look.

276) Plan three quick meals

Yes, I love food and dinner is often the highlight of my day, so another meal challenge today! On your phone, note down three different dishes you can make on a weeknight and the ingredients you need to make them. They should be:

★ Quick and straightforward to make.

★ Not need too many ingredients – and even better if most of the ingredients can be kept for a while without going off.

★ Not be too expensive.

★ Things you actually want to eat!

Having some ideas ready to go for when you are tired and too frazzled to think creatively is so useful. It might save you a stressful wander round the supermarket or stop you ordering a takeaway you don't actually want. Change and update this list as you get bored or discover a new easy weeknight recipe.

277 Keep friends in mind

When you have five minutes today, scroll through texts and WhatsApps. Think about each of your friends for a moment. Do you know what's going on with them? Is anyone going through a tough time? If there's someone who you haven't heard from in a while, drop them a message to say hi and see what's going on with them.

278 Freshen up your living room

I know that some of you will hate me for this, while some of you will enjoy it as much as I do! Have a look round your sofa furnishings – cushion covers, throws, even sofa covers sometimes – and see what can go in the washing machine. Now check again it can *definitely* go in the washing machine before you put it in! If you throw in some lovely fabric softener, not only will your cushions, etc. look clean and refreshed, your whole home will smell like it's been through the washing machine for a few days too. And we all need a refresh from time to time.

(279) Celebrate!

It's time to celebrate all those lovely wins. What has felt good for you? Did you manage to do something you thought you'd find challenging? Did you feel uncomfortable at any point but pushed through it anyway? Was there anything you were dreading but that actually turned out OK?

Choose your theme #11

It's time to pick another theme. You can return to something you chose earlier in the book if you like, or perhaps something along the same lines? What theme have you felt was the most useful for you so far?

MY THEME IS

281 The no-shopping solution

A while ago, you cleared out all the clothes that don't fit you and you repaired anything that needed it – hopefully your wardrobe is feeling like a slightly less cluttered and calmer thing to stand in front of! So today's challenge is to put together a new outfit from what you already have. Or at least to remind yourself to wear things together that you don't usually.

282 The shopping solution

When you were looking through your clothes yesterday, did you notice any 'gaps'? For example, did you think, *I'd wear that skirt so much more if I had a navy T-shirt to go with it, and that would go with a load of other stuff too.* Today, before you forget, make a note of those things to remind you when you next go shopping. I know it's less fun than buying a fab new dress or something, but if you get the basics covered then it does make it a lot easier to get dressed and make the most of the stuff you already have.

283 Walk through a worry

This is a bit like what we did with 'Stressbusting' on Day 242. It's so easy to get swamped by worries sometimes – particularly when we're tired and stressed. It can be tough to see a way through, but I think proactively asking ourselves a few questions about the thing/s we are worried about can help. It won't make the problem magically go away, but if it makes it just a little easier to cope with it's worth it.

★ Do I know what it is exactly I am worried about?

★ How likely is it to happen?

★ What would I do if it did happen?

★ Is there anything I can do now to make it feel less worrying?

★ Have I shared my worry with anyone? Who would be the best person to talk to?

★ What would I advise someone else to do if they were worried about a similar thing?

★ What is worrying about this doing to me? Is there any way to let go of the worry a little or turn it into positive action?

284 What's in the fridge?

If you're at home right now, go and have a look in the fridge. How much fruit and veg do you have in? What are your favourites and how often do you buy them? It's much easier to eat well for your body if you have some good veggies that you actually like to hand – and an idea of what you can make with them. So if you have loads of broccoli, for example, and you're out of ideas, take a moment to Google recipes and see if you can find something quick and easy you might not have thought of.

285 Today, I am grateful for . . .

It's time to take a breath and think about all the positives. What lovely things are you grateful for? Write them below:

_____

_____

_____

_____

It's much easier
to eat well for your
body if you have
some good veggies
that you actually
like to hand

286 What does good mental health feel like for you?

When you feel good, how do you feel? I know, it might seem like a stupid question, but do take a minute to think about it. For me, when my mental health is really good I bounce out of bed with so much energy, get loads done without putting it off and I don't let anything faze me. It's important to think about this because this is the real you. Any periods of poor mental health do not define you. Your lowest point is not who you are – what you have written here, that is who you are.

_____

_____

_____

_____

_____

_____

287 What are your mental health warning signs?

I think most of us are aware when we are suffering a period of poor mental health. It's definitely not something I wouldn't notice! But how good are you at seeing the little changes of mood or habits that can indicate that you might need to turn up the self-care? Do you make less effort to see your friends? Sleep more? Stop exercising? If you are feeling well enough today, write them down to hopefully help you consciously notice them in future so you can try to do something that makes you feel better. I know – it won't always work. But it's all about knowing ourselves as well as we can and taking care of ourselves to the best of our abilities.

288 Mental health checklist

Let's think about what you wrote down yesterday and turn it into something practical. You might want to adapt this to suit your brain, but for me these are the main areas which have an effect on my mental health. The idea is that you can give yourself a tick if you have done the thing over the past few days. Keep coming back to this list (colour in that star if you like!), and if you are regularly not ticking one or more boxes you can use it as a reminder to pay some attention to that area.

☐ I have done some exercise or walked somewhere

☐ I've chatted to friends

☐ I've laughed out loud

☐ I've eaten some things that are good for me

☐ I've been getting enough sleep

☐ I've found times to take moments for myself rather than always rushing around

289 Write a note to yourself for when you're feeling low

If your mental health is good right now, how about writing a note to Future You to read when you are not feeling so great? The main thing is to remind yourself of all the positives (you might want to look back at the Celebrate! days we have been doing once a month or your gratitude lists). Try not to tell Future You what they should be doing too much, if you don't think this would help. Focus on being kind – we all deserve kindness, especially you when you are feeling low. Put it in an envelope and keep it somewhere safe.

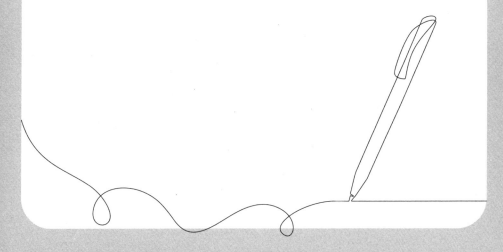

290 Your creative outlet

When we were kids, we could pass hours drawing, playing with plasticine, making up stories, but we don't always make time for the creative parts of our brains when we grow up and life gets busy. Getting absorbed in a project is so good for our mental health. What are the top ways you like to be creative? Even if you don't see yourself as an arty person, there will still be ways that you enjoy being creative. Do you like gardening, DIY, doing online make-up tutorials, playing Minecraft . . .? These are all creative things, too! Today, think about what your creative outlets are – however big or small – and try to find at least ten minutes to do one of them.

291 The people I love

Who are the people who are most important to you? Whose love and support are you grateful to have in your life? (Dogs and other fur babies absolutely count, too!) Write them down here. Don't forget that they are the people you can reach out to if you are struggling. One of the hardest things about going through a period of bad mental health is that it can make you feel isolated and lonely. It's so important to get the support you need – these are the people who will be there.

---

292 An honest conversation

Looking at the list you made yesterday of all the people you love, who do you feel you can talk most openly to about how you feel? In recent years, the stigma around poor mental health and mental illness has been broken down loads, which is amazing. But a lot of us still have the tendency to bottle things up. We can all make a difference to making the world kinder and it even easier to have conversations about mental health by being open about our own feelings when we feel safe to do so. And also by asking other people how they are and really listening to their answers.

293 Go for dinner on your own

OK, I don't know how you feel about it but this was a big one for me. Until recently, I had never eaten dinner out by myself and always thought I would feel really self-conscious and awkward. I have deliberately put this near the end of the book, so if you do feel like I did, hopefully you have built up some confidence and willingness to give things a go by now! The truth is, no one cares if you are out on your own for dinner. If they think about it at all, they will probably assume you are a high-powered businesswoman on her way back to her hotel after closing a deal! Obviously I'd rather have dinner with my partner, H, but there is something empowering about knowing you have the confidence to sit in a restaurant by yourself.* Spending time on our own is not something that comes naturally to all of us, but it is a kind of superpower, in my opinion.

(*I'd still take a book or a magazine, though!!)

(294) TWO-WEEK CHECK-IN!

You are halfway through your theme. How's it going? Have you been able to reflect on it? Today, think about if there is any practical action you'd like to take, if you haven't already. Is there anything you'd like to try out or change?

(295) Learn something interesting (and share it!)

It's entirely up to you what this is, so get your thinking cap on. What are you interested in? A historical figure? A particular animal? Something from the world of science? Look it up on the internet and see if you can find one really cool fact about it that you didn't know. And then tell someone about it. If we have a conversation about something, we are much more likely to remember it. (You can write it down here too, if you like.)

296 Go to a library

I love that just anyone can walk into a library and hang out there as long as they want without having to buy anything, as you would have to if you wanted to sit in a coffee shop, for example. If you can, try to go to a library today and have a browse. Sign up for membership if you're not already a member – you usually only need some ID and proof of address.

297 Change it up

What might you do this weekend? Can you do that tonight or tomorrow night instead? I think we can get into a pattern where we just think fun is mainly for weekends and we don't plan anything for weeknights. So if you can, mix it up a bit and see if you can bring some fun to weekdays too.

298 New music

Just like with anything, it's easy to get stuck in a rut with music, and while it's great to have the old favourites that make you want to dance around your bedroom, it's also good to discover new things too. So today your mission is to find at least one singer or band you're not familiar with to listen to. Try out recommendations on your streaming service or ask friends or colleagues what they are into at the moment.

299 Compliments

All the way back on Days 96 and 200, you wrote down some compliments you have received. Have a flick back now and read over them. Have you had any more good compliments recently? Do you think you've gotten any better at accepting compliments and not brushing it off when people say nice things?

300 Compliment a stranger

Let's stay on compliments. Today's job is to find a way to compliment someone you don't know! I know, it could be a challenge, particularly if you don't love speaking to strangers. But I'm pretty sure you've got this. The two important things to remember: it has to be sincere and how they react is out of your control. All you can do is say something nice. What they do with that is up to them.

301 Cold-water therapy (part three!)

It's that time again! Hopefully you've been finding a blast of cold water is really refreshing and maybe even good for your mental health, like I do, but even if you're not convinced, will you give it one last try? Challenge yourself to see if you can stand under the cold water for a little bit longer this time.

302

VISION BOARD!
Your choice . . .

We've done six visions boards now! How have you found them? Has the daydreaming led to anything real in your life, or have you just enjoyed imagining the perfect holiday or a brilliant Saturday with your friends? Today, it's time to do another vision board but this time you get to choose. What area of your life would you like to focus on? Where might a little bit of imagination help?

303 Good habit #3

An easy one today – I just want to check in with you to see how your new habits went. Even if they didn't exactly stick, that's OK. Did you learn anything along the way about what works for you and what doesn't? It's important to remember that you are not a project that must be constantly worked on – you are amazing as you are. If there is something you want to change, then you have the power to do so – you just have to find a way that works for you. And it has to come from you and be for you, not anyone else.

304 Say yes to something you'd usually say no to

Today is all about giving something a chance that you'd usually dismiss. It can be anything – a food you wouldn't normally try, an invite you'd usually turn down . . . We tell ourselves 'I can't' or 'I don't' so often – it can feel amazing when that turns into 'I can' and 'I do'! Of course, you know your own comfort levels, so follow your instinct and don't feel you have to do anything you really don't want to. This is about keeping an open mind and not limiting yourself.

305 Say no to something you'd usually say yes to

Today is sort of the opposite of yesterday. Whereas yesterday was about pushing at the edges of your comfort zone, today is about respecting our boundaries. If someone asks you to do something that you don't want to, or you feel it's not really fair, then try to find a way to push back, honestly and politely.

306 Learn about first aid

The idea of someone having an accident is really scary. How confident are you that you'd know what to do? This is a really good example of how we can turn a worry into positive action. Try to take some time today to learn what to do in common first aid scenarios. Like someone burning themselves, having a fit, fainting, etc. The UK-based St John Ambulance has loads of good advice on their website.

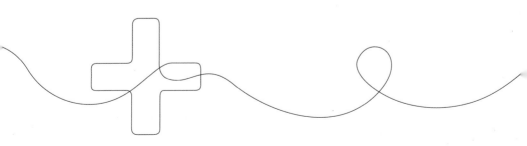

(307) Celebrate!

It's time to celebrate all your wins and reflect on all the things that have gone well. What was your favourite this month?

_____

_____

_____

_____

_____

_____

_____

Choose your theme #12

We've still got nearly two months of *One Win a Day* left, but this is the last theme I'm going to ask you to pick. Of course, if you've found it helpful you can carry this habit on in whatever way feels good to you. So what's it going to be?

MY THEME IS

_____

309 Check your diary

What do you have coming up in the next month that you are looking forward to? Do you have any quiet weeks when you could plan something fun? Time can go by so quickly and just dealing with the day-to-day can be so consuming that it's easy to forget to stop and look ahead. So this is your challenge for today!

310 A crafty gift

On Day 290 you started exploring something a bit crafty. Now let's take this to the next level and share it with the world! Give something you've made as a gift to someone else – whether that's a meal, a cake, a drawing or a bit of knitting, it doesn't matter. It's the fact it's been made with care and love. And the reaction you get to it will give you the warm fuzzies, too.

311 Go outside for five minutes first thing

If you can do this at dawn, that would be amazing. But if that's five o'clock in the morning for you right now, then I'll let you off. If you have a dog you might do this anyway, but if you don't you can still make time to appreciate the early morning! As soon as you're up, chuck on some clothes and go for a very quick walk. If you need an incentive, you can go and get a coffee or some juice. There is something really nice and calming about being out and about first thing, I always think. It feels like you are starting the day on the right foot and you don't have to rush to catch up with it.

(312) Keep a diary #1

I used to keep a diary when I was younger. I think it's a great thing for kids and young people to do when you're trying to make sense of how you feel and the world around you. I have never tried journaling as I'm not sure it's really my thing (though of course I should try it to find out!), but lots of people find it so helpful for their mental health. This week, consider keeping some form of diary or journal if you don't already, just to see how it feels. It's up to you what format this takes. You might want to write about your feelings that day and/or what happened, or perhaps you want to focus on gratitude or recording positive things. Decide what format you want your diary to take but try to keep the entries short – if you are too ambitious it might start to feel like a chore.

313 Say 'Yes, but . . .'

It's OK to have negative thoughts – it's actually totally unavoidable! It's not like everything is going to be unicorns and cupcakes every day. Today, though, I want you to be conscious of your negative thoughts. Acknowledge them, but rather than dwelling on them or pretending that everything is fine, accept that is how you feel – but try to add a positive thing too. For example, you might think, *YES, today is Monday and I'm not looking forward to facing my annoying boss,* and then add, *BUT on Wednesday I'm seeing my best friend.* Or, *BUT I'm starting to apply for new jobs.* Or even, *BUT I do know my boss means well and they were really kind/helpful when this thing happened. So they aren't all bad.*

314 Have a day off caffeine

If you're a big coffee or tea drinker, then this might be the most controversial suggestion I'll make! How does it feel to take caffeine out of your life? What can you replace it with? A day isn't enough to wean yourself off caffeine (it can take up to nine days to get over the withdrawal symptoms!), but it might be interesting to know what the you without caffeine is like!

315 Grow something (for free!)

This is a fun one to do with kids, but even if you don't have any living in your house I still think you can give it a go! Loads of stuff that we throw away can actually sprout and grow if we give it a windowsill and a bit of water. (Not that different to life really – you just have to give things a chance . . .) There's loads about this online, but some examples are:

★ Put some carrot tops in a shallow saucer of water. Within a week they should start to sprout green leaves which you can sprinkle over a salad.

★ Rest the bottom of an avocado stone in a jar of water. When it grows roots and a shoot, put it in some compost for a free houseplant!

★ Mint, rosemary and basil are super-easy to grow from a sprig or cutting. Put it in a small jar of water and pot it up when it has a decent set of roots.

★ Poke some cloves of garlic into a pot of compost. The long green shoots that pop up are like garlicky chive – you can chop them up and use them as a garnish.

316   **Find out about volunteering**

You may well not have any time available to volunteer – that's absolutely fine. All I'd like you to do is to think about *if* you did have time, what might you be interested in doing? And then do a bit of research to find out what sort of opportunities are available in your local area. It's always good to be reminded that there are lots of amazing people out there giving up their time to help others. And, now, if you find you have some time on your hands and you want to become one of them, you have a bit more of an idea of what you might do . . .

317   **Go to a pub quiz**

Or plan to host one with your friends if pubs aren't really your thing. Do you remember in the lockdowns when lots of people were doing quizzes all the time?! It feels so long ago, but it's fun to get your brain working and test your general knowledge!

318 Eat lunch while looking at nature

If it's a lovely summer's day where you are, then this will be easy – take your sandwiches straight to the park or garden! If it's cold you might want to sit indoors, but is there somewhere you can go where you can still see nature? If you can barely see a tree from where you are this lunchtime, you might have to get creative! For example, Google 'world's best views' or 'mountains photos' and daydream about when you can next get outdoors . . .

319 Keep a diary #2

It's been a week since you started experimenting with writing a diary. How did you find it? Does writing about any particular area of your life help you see more clearly? You don't have to commit to keeping a diary every day if you don't want to. Using a paper and pen to help you sort through your feelings is a useful tool and you can do it whenever you like.

320 Bring something from the outside, inside

This is admittedly going to be harder if it's winter when you're reading this, but it's still totally doable. In fact, it makes it even more interesting. It could just be some flowers from the garden (too easy!), but think outside the box. What about some shells if you live near the sea, some interesting leaves (particularly if it's autumn) or a beautiful feather? Anything that catches your eye. The point is that a) you're going to have to get outdoors to do this, and b) you'll have to really look at your surroundings to find something cool enough to take indoors.

321 Find out someone's name

I bet there's someone you see around quite often whose name you don't know. The server in a café, someone in your work canteen, a neighbour you sort of wave to? Today, ask them what their name is. Don't worry if you feel bad for not knowing – you are going to fix that!

322 TWO-WEEK CHECK-IN!

You are halfway through your theme. How's it going? Have you been able to reflect on it? Today, think about if there is any practical action you'd like to take, if you haven't already. Is there anything you'd like to try out or change?

323 Bargain hunt

Try to pop into a local charity shop today and see if you can find anything that catches your eye. I went through a phase where I kept buying vases in charity shops to upcycle. To be honest, it got a bit ridiculous and I ended up with loads! But I do love a good charity shop and it's amazing what you can find. You get the satisfaction of not buying new all the time – better for the planet – and giving your money to a good cause rather than Mr Amazon for a change.

324 Shake it out!

Have you ever noticed the way dogs do a massive shake sometimes? It can be because they have too much excess energy – like they have been playing and got a bit wound up – and need to reset themselves. I think humans can benefit from this! If you're feeling stressed or a bit hyped up about something and want to calm your brain and body a bit, make like a dog and jump up and down, then shake all your limbs out! You can do it to music if you like (so if anyone asks, you can say you were dancing!). You might want to finish off with the box breathing (Day 32) or forward fold (Day 103) if you want to chill a bit afterwards.

325 Today, I am grateful for . . .

It's time to take a breath and think about all the positives. This is the last time I'm going to ask you to do this in *One Win a Day*, so have a really good think and also take the opportunity to flick back and remind yourself of what you have been grateful for over the course of the year. (You can find the gratitude lists on Days 5, 46, 73, 94, 131, 169, 208, 256 and 285.)

_____

_____

_____

_____

_____

_____

_____

_____

_____

326 Sort out your handbag

Or work bag, or school bag, or whatever bag you use most often. Take everything out of it, shake out all the fluff and dirt and wipe the outside free of any dust. Is there anything in there that shouldn't be? Do you need to carry around three nail files and half a squashed KitKat?! Is there anything that you always need but never have? Lip balm, tissues, chewing gum, a mirror . . .?

327 Clean your make-up brushes . . .

. . . make-up bag, hairbrush. While we're having a bit of a clean, let's do make-up brushes and hairbrushes. This is the sort of job that you would ideally do regularly as dirt does accumulate and you want to put nice clean things on your beautiful face and in your hair. But, let's be honest here, who remembers to do this as much as they should? So today, let's get it done and ticked off the list!

328 Gather all those bits of paper

It's so much easier now most stuff is online, but bits of paper do still accumulate. Do a walk-through of the house today and grab any homeless bits of paper – newspapers and magazines and junk mail included. Recycle anything you don't need so you're just left with a small pile of things you do need or want to hang on to.

329 Admin blitz

This is boring but you will feel good when it's out of the way. See if you can allocate half an hour to this today. First, grab all those documents you decided to hold on to yesterday and file them. As you're doing that, take the opportunity to look through and see if there's anything you need to action. When is your phone contract up? What about the car insurance? Do you need to renew any railcards or switch to another energy supplier? Make yourself a list, put important dates in the diary as a reminder if you need to, and if you have any time left from the half-hour you gave yourself, see if you can get one simple thing done.

Ask for help OR get it sorted

There are two options for today, and deciding which is for you requires a bit of self-knowledge. And we're always wanting to know ourselves better, right?

If you're someone who's really independent and likes to be able to do things for themselves, identify a task or something that's holding you back in your own life and think of someone who might be able to help you with it. Approach them and ask for help.

If you feel like you often turn to others for help, try figuring out something by yourself today. You might need to Google some videos or do a bit of research, but try to tackle a job you usually wouldn't. If you give it a good go and you still find you need help, then that's fine. The point is to have a go.

331 Find out something you didn't know about your area

Who is that statue of? What actually is that unusual building you walk past all the time? How old is your town and why is it there? Whether you've just moved or you've lived in the same place for most of your life, get curious and see if you can find out a couple of cool facts. You might see your home in a whole new light . . .

332 Get clued up on your energy usage

Thinking about what the energy-hungry things are in your home can help you save money and lower your carbon footprint, all for minimal effort. When you know what is eating your power you might choose to do things differently. For example, washing machines, dishwashers and tumble driers use lots of power, so you might decide to wash at a lower temperature and only use them when you have a full load. There's a load of information online, for example on www.energysavingtrust.org.uk

333 Talk to someone you don't know

Try to strike up a short conversation with at least one stranger today. The server in a coffee shop is the easiest (if it's not busy) as it's sort of their job to be nice to customers! But really, anybody will do . . . The point is to remember that if you reach out to someone, you've done a good thing. Some people will respond really well and love it that you've started a conversation. Sometimes they will be having a bad day, be really shy or, let's be honest, be a bit of a dickhead and they won't want to engage. There's nothing you can do about that. If they are a stranger, they don't know you. So their bad manners or shyness is nothing to do with you.

334 Two ten-minute jobs

Do you remember the three five-minute jobs challenge? Today, just pick a couple of things that take up to ten minutes that have been hanging around your to-do list for a while. Take a deep breath, think about how great it will be to give yourself a big fat tick for each of them – and get them done!

335 Celebrate your favourite wins

This is the last time we're going to do this, so let's make it count. Feel free to record all the things that have felt good over the last four weeks, but I'd also love you to flick back through the eleven previous times you've made a note of all your wins. First, take a moment to think about how awesome and strong you are. You have done ALL that in less than a year! Now reflect on what made you feel especially good. I'm sure there will be some big things on this list, but deliberately try to pick some that might not be things you'd shout about to other people but that meant something to you. It's just another way to remind ourselves that a win is a win, and you are the only person who can decide what matters in your life.

336 Your least-favourite wins

And again, let's find the positive in the negatives. Today, think about what 'wins' you have loved less. Did you hate trying to sit still for a whole ten minutes? Did it feel weird to have dinner out on your own? Remember, no one is expecting you to be perfect. Not everything will go to plan all the time. And that's FINE. Actually, it's better than fine, because even the things that don't go so well give us an opportunity to reflect and learn more about ourselves. That's a win too, right?

_____

_____

_____

_____

_____

_____

_____

337 Get some photos printed

What photos did you put in your inspiration folder? I bet you have some really nice ones of your friends and family in your phone somewhere. Order some physical prints online to refresh your photo displays at home. And order a couple of extras of those with friends or family members, too . . .

338 Do an online tutorial

What would you like to learn how to do? French plait, put up shelves, make sushi? See if you can find some tutorials that will teach you to do just that. Some YouTube videos will be better than others, so you might have to try a few. Bookmark or save the links to the ones you think will be most useful.

Learn about love languages

You might have heard of this. Love languages are the different ways people express love – to their partner but friends and family too. They are: acts of service (as in, doing nice things for someone to show you care), giving gifts, spending quality time, words of affirmation (telling them you love them, how they make you feel) and physical touch. Knowing what yours are (most people tend to feel most comfortable with a couple of them at least) is interesting.

It's also helpful to understand the love language of the people you have relationships with. For example, you might wonder why your partner doesn't tell you how they feel about you very often, but for them, every time they make you a cup of tea or bring you chocolate back from the shops they are saying they love you. There's loads online about it and I think it's really interesting.

340 The year I was born

How much do you know about what was going on in the world the year that you arrived in it? Do you know what was number one and what the big issues of the day were? Even what was the most popular TV show or Christmas toy that year! Take five minutes to find out more . . .

341 Post some photos

When your photos from Day 337 arrive, pick out a few of the spares and post them to the people who are in those photos, too. You might like to include a short note to say why you like the photo so much and why you chose to print it. Getting a lovely photo in the post out of the blue would be a wonderful surprise.

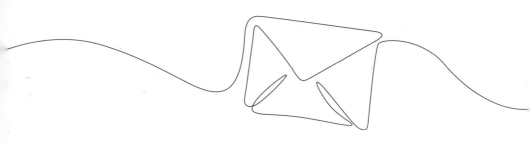

(342) Treat yourself!

I have set you some big challenges over the past few weeks and you know what? Everyone needs a day off! Today, I just want you to treat yourself to something – a new top, a bath, a takeaway – whatever your heart desires. Because you are awesome and you absolutely bloody deserve it!

(343) Have a chat with someone much older or younger than you

If you can today, try to have a conversation with someone of a different generation. It doesn't have to be deep or heavy, but try to ask their opinion on something and really listen to their perspective. Notice where it's different to yours, or not what you would have expected.

344 Learn about the STOP technique

When we are busy and stressed, everything builds up and can feel like it's pressing down on us. Our brain can feel like it's constantly on high alert, which makes it so hard to take a moment and get some perspective. This is where this exercise comes in. It's basically taking mental time out.

S = stop. Whatever you are doing, just put it down for a moment and walk away.

T = take a few deep breaths. Try to only think about the air going in and out of your lungs.

O = observe. What are you thinking and feeling right now? Whatever it is, it's OK. Just naming your emotions can help sort out the jumble in your head. Your thoughts aren't facts and they aren't permanent, remember. You're not going to always feel like this.

P = proceed. Try to do something small that will make you feel better in that moment. For example, talk to a friend, make yourself a cup of tea, go for a walk.

345   What's in season?

Just a quick little task for today. What time of year is it and what fruit and veg is especially good right now where you are? Eating stuff at the time of year it's at its best is a good idea, not just because it will taste better but it's often cheaper as there will be a lot of it around. Plus it's another nice way to connect ourselves to nature and remind us of the changing seasons.

346   Check in with your body

How are you feeling? Wide awake or sluggish and tired? Any aches and pains? Find ten minutes today to run a full body scan in your head. What might make you feel better? For example, if your back feels scrumpled from long hours sitting at a desk, do you need to try to get up and move around and stretch more often? If you feel bloated, is there anything you could try to improve your gut health? Make a note of anything that needs your attention.

(347) Easy wins

We are so near the end of *One Win a Day* and you have come so far! Today, all I want you to do is to flick back through the book and pick some simple wins you enjoyed. Did you like making vision boards? Did spending time away from your phone in the evening or taking a day off social media help your mental health? Try to find eight of the wins that made a difference to you and that you want to go back to in the future. Make a note here or in your diary or journal if you have one, so they are easy to find again when you need a reminder.

1 _____

2 _____

3 _____

4 _____

5 _____

6 _____

7 _____

8 _____

(348) Make your favourite dinner from when you were a kid

This is a fun Friday challenge, so feel free to swap this to a Friday if you prefer and do something else today. As I've said before, it can be enjoyable to reconnect with all the passions you had as a kid, before you became a self-conscious teenager and maybe thought a bit more about what was 'cool'. And taste and smell can be such powerful reminders. So what was your favourite dinner when you were little and how can you re-create it now? (If you used to love Turkey Twizzlers and are now a veggie, then this might be more of a challenge and you might need to pick something else!)

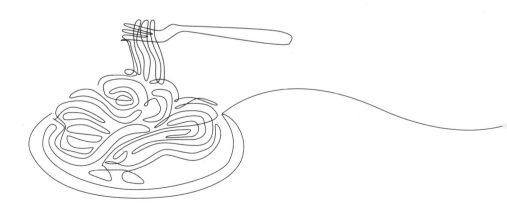

349 Sort your jewellery

Do you have a tangled mess of a jewellery box or a few pieces stored neatly away? Take some time today to go through your jewellery. Decide if there is a better way to store it and get rid of anything that is broken beyond repair. Give away things you know for sure you won't wear again and clean any silver or gold that needs it. You may even find some pieces you'd forgotten about that you can start wearing again.

350 A moment that made you

Today, try to find some time to consider a moment that, with hindsight, really shaped who you are today. It could be big or small, but try to think of something positive. What happened and why was it so meaningful? Did it teach you something, show you a new possibility, change your mind about something? I think that the big, headline things that happen to us are obviously important, but we are also shaped by lots of quieter moments too.

351 Canvass some opinions . . .

There are two parts to this one. First, think of a decision you have been considering recently. It's best if it's more of a practical thing than emotional – like where to go on holiday, whether to get a different car, change the colour of your hair or revamp a room. Choose a few people to ask what they think you should do. You might be surprised by their answers! Take a bit of time to think over the advice you've been given.

352 . . . but know your own mind!

Think back to the answers you got yesterday. Try to notice if you felt swayed by someone else's opinion, and why that was. How easy do you find it to consider someone else's views but still know what you think? Did you change your mind because of who they were, or because their advice genuinely feels like a better option? Hopefully you are surrounded by wise and caring people who can give you useful insights into all sorts of things. But, ultimately, we always need to stay connected to who we are and what we want.

353 Learn about money

I know, I don't love having to sort out financial stuff either. But I have learned (the hard way!) that putting your head in the sand is not a good idea. The best thing we can do for our financial health (and stress levels!) is to try to understand money and bills. So whatever is at the forefront of your mind or to-do list where your finances are concerned, spend some time today trying to get your head around it. Whether it's mortgages, credit cards, insurance, savings accounts . . . Knowing more about how something works will always make you feel more confident and in control.

354 Plan a reward

OK, yesterday was a lot! Today, I want you to think of something lovely to do (or maybe something you've been wanting to buy yourself) and figure out a time when you can do that. If you make a note to remind yourself, it will help you to focus on giving yourself the little treat you deserve.

355 Cwtch!

Cwtch is the Welsh word for 'snuggle'. Whether it's your dog, your partner, a lovely soft duvet – find something or somebody nice to *cwtch* today! If you don't have any fur babies of your own, then borrow someone else's for a minute. We all need a hug sometimes.

356 Choose a motto

The Hogwarts' motto is '*Draco dormiens nunquam titillandus*', which means 'Never tickle a sleeping dragon'. What do you want yours to be? Pick something meaningful to you – funny or serious – and write it in big letters somewhere. Remind yourself of it when you need a bit of a boost. Here are some ideas if you need inspiration:

- ★ *Seize the day*

- ★ *Things only change if I change them*

- ★ *Keep on keeping on*

- ★ *There is nothing to fear but fear itself*

- ★ *One thing at a time*

- ★ *I've got this*

357 VISION BOARD! Life

For the very last vision board of the book I want you to go nuts and let your mind go wherever it feels inspired. Create a new Pinterest board or get out the scissors and glue – whatever you're in the mood for. Grab a load of images that speak to you and the life you want to lead. As ever, don't forget that your present life already has so much good stuff in it. So think about representing the things you most love right now on the board, too, alongside your wildest daydreams!

358 Make an appointment

Are you due a trip to the dentist? Is your smear test overdue? Have you been meaning to make a doctor's appointment to address an issue you are having? Today is the day to try to get that sorted! You only get one body and it's an amazing thing that needs to be looked after. It's easy to let these things fall off the to-do list when we are busy, but they are so important.

359 Clean the windows

You don't need to go up a ladder or anything – only the ones you can reach. Let's let some light and clarity in and remind ourselves to stop and admire the view sometimes!

360 Find your tribe

Whatever you are into – adventure travel, sci-fi films, baking – go online and spend some time finding blogs, social media accounts and other spaces where people who have the same passion are sharing their ideas and stories. It's a great way to get some inspiration and remind yourself that there are lots of people out there who are into the same things as you, even if your family think you're weird because you know every word of every Disney film!

361 'This is AMAZING!'

I really use this word a lot! But I don't care – it's a great word. Maybe 'awesome' or 'bloody brilliant' is your go-to. Whatever it is, I want you to say it out loud as much as you can today. To your partner when they make you tea. To a colleague when they are helpful. To your kids when they find their own shoes for once! About a nice sandwich at lunchtime. Definitely to yourself in the mirror before you leave the house. Let's face it, not everything in life goes the way we want, so let's recognize and celebrate everything that *is* good. Even if it's only a ham and cheese panini from Costa.

362 Choose your own win

I'm betting that after nearly a whole year of *One Win a Day* you've pretty much got the hang of it by now! So it's your turn. What do you want to do today? Choose your very own win and go out there and do it.

363 Oscars acceptance speech

OH MY GOD, YOU WON! They've opened the envelope and it's official: you got the Oscar, the Booker Prize, the Nobel Peace Prize, whatever your imagination desires! First of all, what are you wearing? A sexy red dress? A sharply cut tux? Now I want you to imagine what you are going to say and who you are going to thank. What are all the things that have helped make you so amazing?

364 It's still all about you

The very first thing I challenged you to do was to think about all the things that are important to you and what makes you, you. Go back to Day 1 and look at this list. Do you still feel the same about the things on it? Do you want to add or change anything? You are unique and special and capable of so much – I hope you know you have proved it over these past 364 days. And at the same time, you are also constantly learning and growing. So please take a moment to celebrate who you have been, who you are now and all the wins – *all* of them – you've had along the way.

**You are unique
and special and
capable of so
much!**

(365) What's next?

I am not one for five-year plans or anything like that.
I try to keep inspired and looking forward to the
future, but having a rigid set of goals is just not me.
Maybe that's you too, or perhaps you get excited by
mapping out where you want to go next. Whatever
your own style, on the very last day of this book,
I'd love for you to think about what's next. What is
coming up on your horizon? What would you like
more of? What possibilities make you feel excited
butterflies in your stomach? Whatever it is, I know
you can do it. You are amazing and you've got this.

Thank Yous

Firstly, to my incredible followers who watch and support me every day, I would like to thank you guys for being so supportive. Without you I would never have been able to create this second book, so thank you so much!

Secondly, to Liz Marvin, my wonderful project editor, who is absolutely amazing and laughs at me daily with my made-up words (that apparently can't go into a book?!).

Thank you to Louise Evans who designed these beautiful pages, and Emily Courdelle who created my wonderful book cover. And to Kate, my publisher, and all the super-wonderful team at Transworld for trusting me to do another book with them. We made it! One win at a time!

x